D1607063

The ILLINOIS Adventure

BILL STEPIEN

CHARNELLE LEWIS

JOHN LEWIS

GIBBS·SMITH
P
PUBLISHER

SALT LAKE CITY

07 06 05 04 03 02 01 00   10 9 8 7 6 5

Published by
Gibbs Smith, Publisher
P.O. Box 667
Layton, Utah 84041
1-800-547-9588

Managing Editor: Courtney Johnson

Associate Editors: Susan Myers, Amy Wagstaff

Book design: Kathleen Timmerman

Cover photos: Prairie photo © by Larry Kanfer, (800) 852-6337;
          Chicago photo by Karen I. Hirsch

Printed and bound in Hong Kong

ISBN 0-87905-870-6

This book is dedicated to the young people of Illinois,

about to write new chapters of Illinois history.

What you think and what you do are the building blocks of history.

Build a history in which you can take pride.

CONTENTS

chapter 1

Natural Illinois 2

chapter 2

The First People 26

chapter 3

Claimed by France 44

chapter 4

Illinois Changes Hands 58

chapter 5

Becoming a State 70

chapter 6

The Journey to Illinois 82

chapter 7

Settling Illinois 94

chapter 8

A Time of Troubles 108

chapter 9

The Growth of Chicago 126

chapter 10

A New Century 142

chapter 11

Taking Our Place in the World 158

chapter 12

Our State Government 172

chapter 13

Making a Living in Illinois 186

Glossary 201
Index 205
Credits 213

MAPS

Illinois' Place in the World 5

Illinois' Place in the United States 5

Illinois Cities 6

Tornado Alley 8

Land Regions 14

Major Rivers 19

Ice Age Glaciers in Illinois 22

Illinois and Its Surrounding States 25

Indian Mounds 31

Illini Lands 38

French Claims, 1754 46

Jolliet and Marquette's Route 47

Early French Settlements 50

The French and Indian War 61

Proclamation Line of 1763 62

The Great Lakes Region 63

Clark's Route 66

The Northwest Territory 68

The Illinois Territory 72

The Capitals of Illinois 79

Water Routes to Illinois 87

Sauk and Fox Lands 91

Three Religious Settlements 101

Lake Michigan to the Gulf of Mexico 103

Illinois Railroads, 1856 105

Routes to Freedom 112

Choosing Sides 119

The Chicago Sanitary and Ship Canal 138

Illinois Counties and County Seats 180

ILLINOIS TERRITORY

Springfield

0   25   50   75   100

Illinois State Symbols

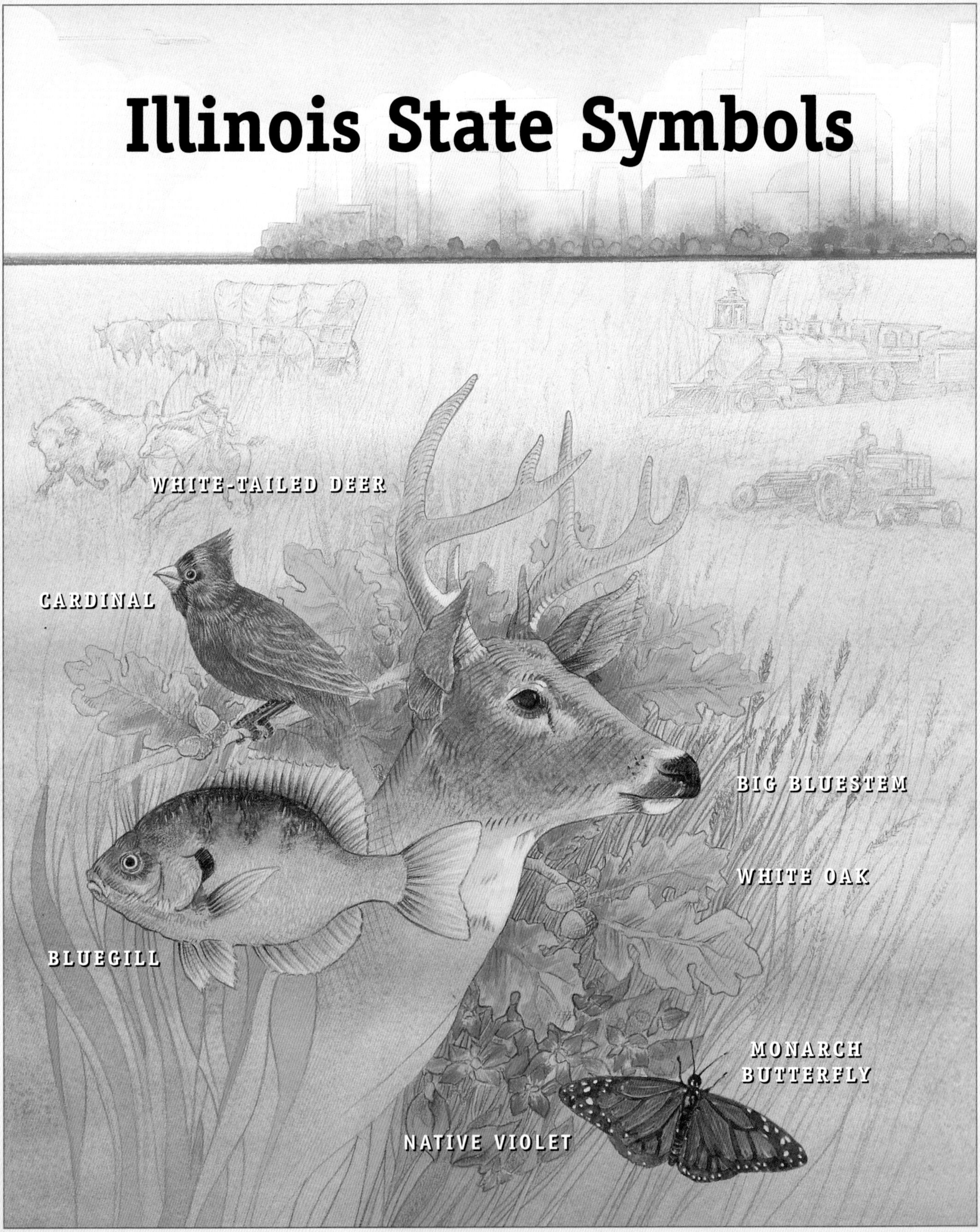

WHITE-TAILED DEER

CARDINAL

BIG BLUESTEM

WHITE OAK

BLUEGILL

MONARCH BUTTERFLY

NATIVE VIOLET

THE ILLINOIS STATE FLAG

The design for our state flag was decided in a contest. The winner was from Rockford. The flag was approved in 1915. Then in 1969 the word "Illinois" was added to the flag. Today the state flag flies at the top of the State Capitol Building in Springfield.

THE ILLINOIS STATE SEAL

Illinois' state seal has changed several times. The first seal was designed when Illinois became a state. Then the eagle and banner were added. On the banner was our state motto: "State Sovereignty, National Union." This means that the state of Illinois has some of its own powers, but it is also part of a larger country or union. After the Civil War, the banner was changed so that the words "National Union" stood out more.

PLACES TO LOCATE
Illinois
North America
United States
Canada
Mexico
Chicago
equator
North and South Poles
Lake Michigan
the Great Lakes
Gulf of Mexico
Mississippi River
Illinois River
Ohio River
Ozark Mountains

TERMS TO UNDERSTAND
geography
continent
temperate
precipitation
migration
organism
ecosystem
particle
nutrient
reservoir
floodplain
tributary
erosion
sod
fertile
adapt
fluorite
scouring
fossil
conserve

chapter 1

Natural Illinois

Starved Rock State Park is near the Illinois River.
(Photo by Tom Till)

These friends are playing at Oak Street Beach in Chicago.

The Land We Call Home

Illinois seems very large. Yet it is just one small part of the world. Because we live in Illinois, it is important to us. It is our home. Millions of people all over the world live in places that are important to them.

In this chapter you will begin to learn about Illinois by studying its *geography*. Geography is the land, water, plants, animals, and people in a place. First we will study where Illinois is located in the world. We will learn what the land is like and how it got that way. We will see how people in Illinois are connected with people all over the world.

Why is it important to know about the geography of a place? Because geography affects where we live and how we live. For example, people live and farm on our flat prairie lands. It is easier to build homes and farm on flat land. Our many lakes and rivers provide water and transportation.

Geographers use five basic themes to talk about the ways geography affects us:

- Location
- Place
- Regions
- Movement
- Relationships within places

LOCATION:
Where in the World Are We?

We all know we live on planet Earth. But just where on planet Earth do we live? Illinois is located on one of the world's *continents*. Continents are very large land areas. They have oceans on many sides. Illinois is on the continent of North America.

Illinois is part of a country on that continent. A country is a land region under the control of one government. Our country is the United States of America. Canada is a country to the north of us. Mexico is a country to the south of us.

Illinois is located at the crossroads of our country. It is a place where north, south, east, and west meet. It was a crossroads for American Indians long before the first white people arrived. More than a hundred years ago, as the railroads were built, Chicago became the transportation center of the nation. Today, when people fly coast to coast they often go through Chicago.

▲ Photo by John D. Ivanko

Illinois' Place in the World

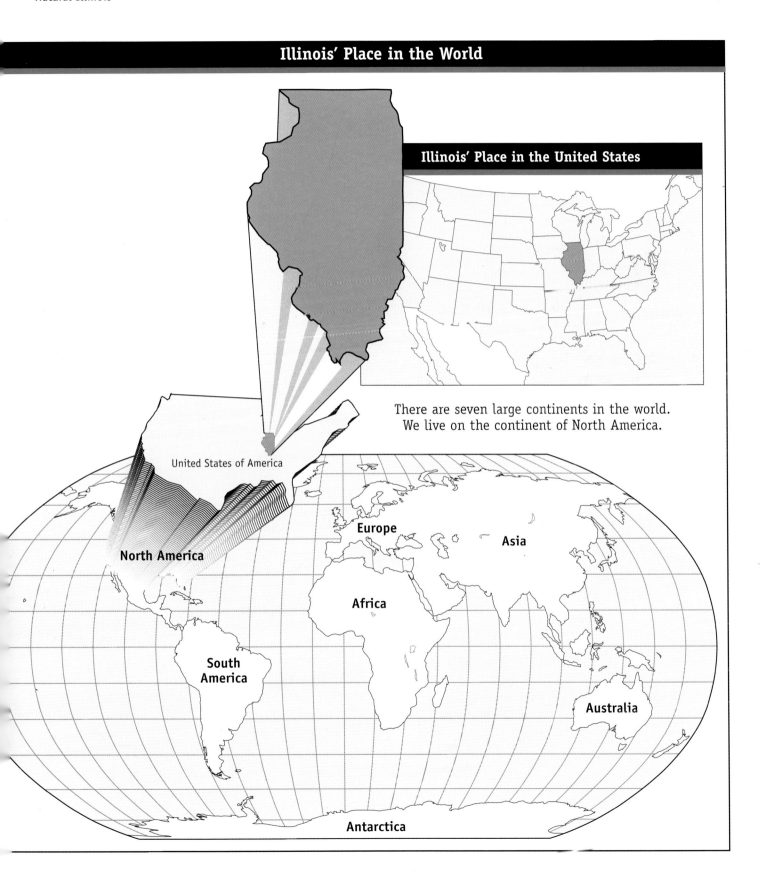

Illinois' Place in the United States

There are seven large continents in the world. We live on the continent of North America.

United States of America

North America

Europe

Asia

Africa

South America

Australia

Antarctica

There are many wonderful places in Illinois.

Cities are built by people.

Rivers are made by nature.

Do you live in one of these cities?

Which cities are closest to you?

Which cities are the farthest away from you?

Are there any rivers near you?

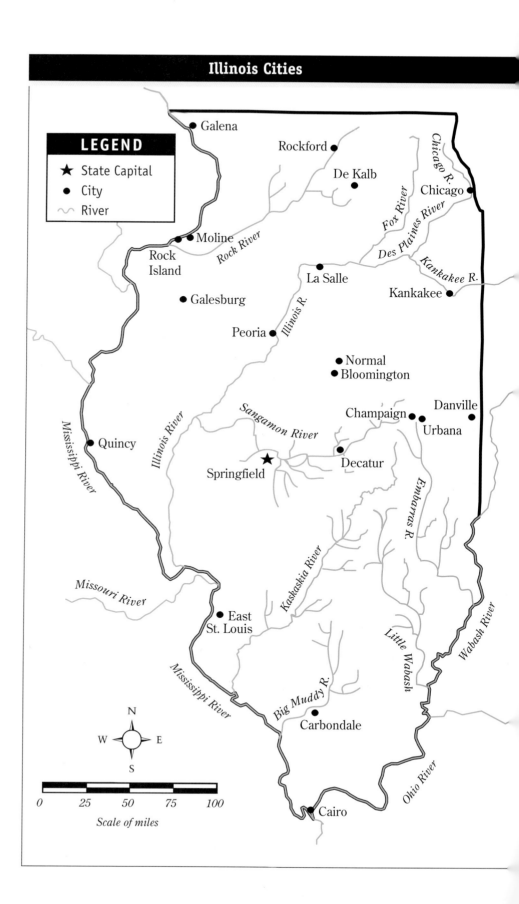

Illinois Cities

LEGEND

★ State Capital

• City

∿ River

PLACE:
What Kind of Place Is Illinois?

▶ Photo by John D. Ivanko

Illinois is a place with forests, lakes, prairies, and rivers. All places have certain features that make them alike or different from other places. Some of these are natural to the environment, such as trees, soil, plant and animal life, rivers, and lakes.

Places also have human features. There are farmhouses with silos. There are tall city buildings. These were made by humans. Freeways, shopping malls, and homes are also examples of human features.

Both natural and human features make up the place we call Illinois.

Our Climate

Climate is also important to a place. Look at where Illinois sits on a map or globe. It is in the middle of North America. It is not close to the equator, where it is warm all year long. It is not close to either the North or South Pole, where it is cold all year long. Illinois is in the *temperate* zone. It is neither hot all year nor cold all year.

Which features shown here are natural? Which are made by people?

▶ Lake Michigan photo by David Blanchette   ▶ Winter scene photo by Karen I. Hirsch

Part of Illinois is near a huge body of water. That's right, it's Lake Michigan. How do you think this affects the climate of Chicago?

Illinois has four seasons: winter, spring, summer, and fall.

What is wind?
Wind is moving air.
Air moves when it is
heated and cooled.
Warm air rises.
Cold air sinks.
This movement
makes wind.

Windmills turn wind into
useful energy.

Can you draw the shape of Illinois? Because our state is so long, summers are hotter in the south than in the north. Temperatures in southern Illinois can reach 105 degrees on summer days. During the winter, temperatures in the north can drop to 35 degrees below zero.

Distance from large bodies of water also helps determine the kind of weather we have. Illinois is far from any ocean, but Chicago is near Lake Michigan. Large bodies of water change temperature more slowly than air does. In the winter, the warmer body of water keeps the nearby land warmer. In summer the cool body of water tends to keep the land cooler.

Land near a large body of water also gets more *precipitation* (rain and snow) than other places. Northern Illinois, near the Great Lakes, gets about 34 inches of precipitation each year. Southern Illinois receives about 41 inches. Its moist air comes from the Gulf of Mexico. The rainfall during the spring and summer is just right for growing corn, wheat, and soybeans.

The land in most of Illinois is level, or flat. The flat land affects the weather. There are no large mountains to slow the wind. Chicago is known as the "Windy City."

▲ Photo by John D. Ivanko

Tornado Alley

Wind can make quick changes in the weather. A strong wind from the south can quickly bring warm moist air into Illinois. A wind from the north can bring cold dry air. That is why tornadoes happen in our state.

A tornado is a violent whirlwind that can cause much damage.

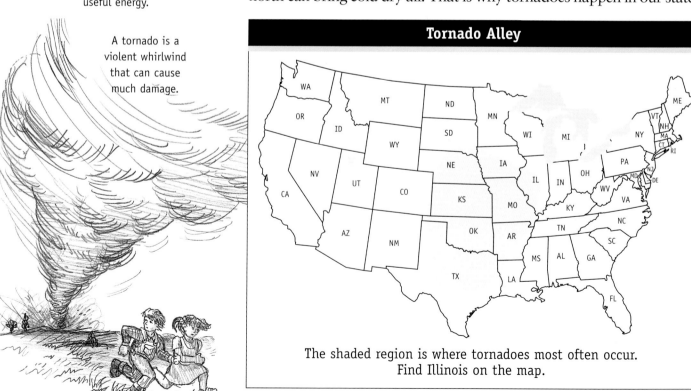

Tornado Alley

The shaded region is where tornadoes most often occur.
Find Illinois on the map.

Illinois sits in a region called Tornado Alley, where warm and cold air often meet. When this happens, the warm air rises. As it rises it forms a spiral and spins. The air around the spiral moves it over the ground.

Most tornadoes move at ten to twenty miles per hour, but they can reach three hundred miles per hour. Some have so much force they pick up cars or houses in their path and whirl them down several miles away.

Tornadoes are very dangerous. Whenever there is a tornado warning it is important to follow safety rules, tune in for information, and get to a safe place quickly.

A Good Place for Farming

Illinois' growing season (the time when there is no frost) is long enough for most grains and vegetables. Our state has rich soil for growing crops. Our many rivers keep the soil drained. It is also a good place to grow crops because the land is level. These things make Illinois a great place for farming.

In fact, agribusiness is one of our biggest industries. Agribusiness is simply agriculture and business put together. Farmers try to figure out the most effective way to raise and sell their crops and livestock. Illinois' leading crops are corn, soybeans, and wheat. Livestock such as hogs and cattle are also important.

agriculture + business = agribusiness

People are not the only ones who love to eat corn. Most of the corn grown in Illinois is used to feed pigs, cattle, and chickens. Some of the corn is also shipped to other countries. Corn is used to make grain alcohol, corn syrup, sugar, and cornstarch. Corn oil is used for cooking and making paint, soap, and other products.

Photos by Karen L. Hirsch

Both animals and plants are part of agribusiness.

The violet is our state flower. It grows naturally throughout most of Illinois.

Owls sleep during the day and hunt for food at night.

Plants provide food for many other life forms. They are the most important part of an ecosystem. People need plants for food, clothing, fuel, shelter, and many other things. We could not survive without grasses and grains.

Plants and Animals

In southern Illinois there are white oak, shingle oak, post oak, sweet gum, river birch, and maple trees. In other parts of the state there are black walnut, honey locust, black cherry, basswood, cottonwood, Kentucky coffee, hickory, ash, and sycamore trees. White pines also grow near White Pine Forest State Park.

Wildflowers include Dutchman's breeches, blue phlox, black-eyed Susans, goldenrods, bluebells, buttercups, prairie docks, blazing stars, and asters.

Have you ever seen a muskrat, mink, weasel, squirrel, wood-chuck (groundhog), raccoon, opossum, skunk, white-tailed deer, beaver, or coyote? These are some of the animals that live in Illinois.

Perhaps you have seen birds flying overhead in the spring and fall. Illinois is located in the Mississippi Flyway, a route followed by millions of birds during their *migrations*. Birds fly south for the winter, then return to the north in the summer.

The Canada goose, merganser, ruddy duck, and mallard can be found in Illinois. The ring-necked pheasant, woodcock, wild turkey, blue jay, American crow, cardinal, ruby-throated hummingbird, sparrow, hawk, owl, thrush, woodpecker, wren, and American bald eagle also make their homes here.

Carp, catfish, bass, freshwater drums, bowfins, suckers, gars, and sunfish swim in our rivers.

Ecosystems

Nature has a way of keeping things in order. Plants and animals get the materials they need from their surroundings. They also give important materials back to the environment. In this way nature keeps things in balance. Plants, animals, and *organisms* interact with each other and with their environment. Each plant or animal depends on the others in order to survive. We call this community an *ecosystem*. You can find ecosystems on land or in lakes, streams, and oceans.

Each ecosystem contains many kinds of life. For example, a prairie is more than just tall grass. There are insects, birds, animals, and even soil *particles*. Each does its own special job.

Some animals are predators, which means they hunt smaller animals. The smaller animals are their prey. The smaller animals eat plants or bugs. The bugs and plants feed on soil which contains nutrients from dead animals. A healthy prairie has enough food sources, predators, and space for its plants and animals.

Ecosystems can be hurt when people or natural changes upset the balance.

Illinois Has Five Natural Ecosystems

Forest
At one time forests covered more of Illinois than they do today. Much of the wildlife in our state lives in the forests.

River and Stream
When people build dams, pollute the water, or bring in animal and plant species from other regions, they can harm the river ecosystem.

Prairie
The small animals eat prairie grasses and flowers. Then larger animals eat the smaller animals. When plants and animals die, their bodies return important *nutrients* to the soil.

Wetland
Wetlands are good for Illinois. They help keep water levels steady when there is heavy rain or melting snow. By absorbing the water, they prevent flooding.

  The wetlands are home to many rare animals.

Lake
You know that rivers are important in Illinois, but did you know that lakes and *reservoirs* are also very important? Most of our drinking water comes from lakes and reservoirs. Fish from lakes are an important source of food.

The Mississippi River

American Indians lived beside the wide Mississippi River, farmed its *floodplains*, fished in it, used it to travel to other villages for trade, and gave it its name. Later, French explorers saw how important the river was for travel and for control of the region.

People of all time periods have used the river. After the pioneers moved west, steamboats paddled up and down the Mississippi. They carried people and goods to budding towns along the river.

Along its course the Mississippi River is joined by many *tributaries*. The Illinois River and the Ohio River are two large tributaries. Over 250 streams and rivers flow through Illinois. These rivers provide water to farms and drain extra water from the soil. They were also a source of power for factories. The rivers form a web of inland waterways through the middle of the United States.

Ducks, geese, swans, warblers, thrushes, woodpeckers, whip-poor-wills, herons, and egrets are just some of the birds that live along the Mississippi River. American bald eagles spend the winter along the river near Nauvoo.

The river is also home to muskrats, minks, beavers, otters, raccoons, skunks, weasels, foxes, gray and fox squirrels, cottontails, jack rabbits, and white-tailed deer.

Over 200 kinds of fish live in the Mississippi River. There are many varieties of catfish alone.

The famous American writer Mark Twain lived next to the mighty Mississippi. He was a riverboat pilot. He called the river "a wonderful book" with stories and secrets to tell.

▲ Photos by John D. Ivanko

Steamboats brought goods and people to growing towns along the river. Today modern bridges cross the river near some of these same towns.

People stop to enjoy the river's natural beauty at Mississippi Palisades State Park.

Beaver

Bald eagle

River otter

REGIONS:
Places with Similar Characteristics

A region is another way to tell about a place. Geographers divide large areas of the world into smaller parts. We call these parts regions. Regions identify places that are alike in some way.

A region can be as large as a continent or as small as your neighborhood. You can live in many regions at the same time. For example, there are political regions, such as your county. You might live in a farming region and watch the corn grow taller than you are each summer. There are mining regions where salt and coal are brought out of the earth. You probably have a favorite recreational region. Even schools are organized into regions called districts. What school district do you live in?

Land Regions

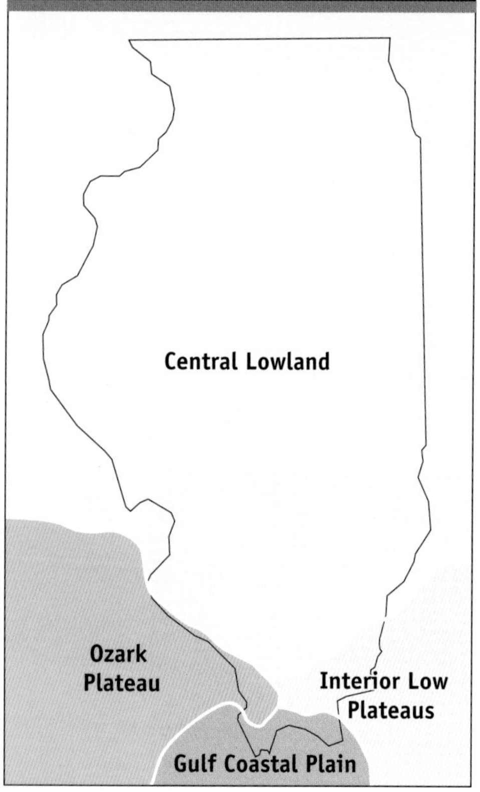

Central Lowland

Ozark Plateau

Interior Low Plateaus

Gulf Coastal Plain

There Are Four Major Land Regions in Illinois

The fertile plains and prairies are perfect for farming.

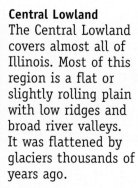

Central Lowland
The Central Lowland covers almost all of Illinois. Most of this region is a flat or slightly rolling plain with low ridges and broad river valleys. It was flattened by glaciers thousands of years ago.

◄ Photo by John D. Ivanko

Shawnee National Forest takes up much of the region.

Interior Low Plateaus
Glaciers never covered the Interior Low Plateaus Region. It has high ridges, bluffs, and hills. You can stand atop a high ridge and look out over the lowlands. It's a great view!

Photo by Karen T. Hirsch

Landforms

A landform is a feature of the earth's surface. Several kinds of landforms are found in Illinois. They are plains, plateaus, bluffs, and ridges. All of these are the result of powerful forces moving inside the earth. They are also the result of wind and water wearing away the earth's surface. This wearing away is called *erosion*.

Ridges are long narrow chains of hills or mountains.

Plateaus are high, wide, flat areas that often end with steep cliffs. They look like tables or wide steps many miles across.

Bluffs are steep cliffs or riverbanks.

Plains are wide level areas of land without many trees.

Ozark Plateau

The Ozark Plateau is a small section of hilly land. This region also has rocky forest land, so not much farming is done here. There is limestone under much of this region. Limestone is an important building material. It is also used to make cement and to improve iron and lead.

Gulf Coastal Plain

The Mississippi and Ohio Rivers have deposited rich soil at the southern tip of Illinois. This region is the Gulf Coastal Plain. It is a small region of very flat land.

The foothills of the Ozark Mountains begin in Illinois.

Horseshoe Lake Fish and Wildlife Area is near Cairo.

▶ Photos by Tom Till

The Prairie

Illinois is nicknamed the "Prairie State." A prairie is a wide, level, grassy land with few trees. Illinois is in the heart of the Tall Grass Prairie Region of the United States.

When European settlers first came to Illinois, over half of the land was covered with tall grass. Many settlers moved on when they came to these grassy lands. They thought that trees did not grow here because the soil was too poor. There was little wood to build their houses.

Some who stayed learned to build a new kind of house. They cut squares of grass, roots, and soil from the land to build *sod* houses. They plowed the grasslands and changed them into farm fields. They learned that the prairie soils were deep and *fertile*. They had found some of the best farmland in North America.

The settlers lived through hot humid summers with biting insects and prairie fires. The winters were cold and windy. But there was great beauty. In early summer the wildflowers formed a sea of color that waved in the wind.

The term "prairie" comes from a French word meaning "meadow."

The settlers called their wagons "prairie schooners." A schooner is a sailing ship. The wagons were given this name because the prairie was like a sea of grass.

▲ Prairie photo by Karen I. Hirsch • Background prairie photo by John Lynn

Each plant and animal plays a special role in prairie life.

▼ Photos by John Lynn

"I see such beauty there. The colors of the flowers at the height of summer;
the song of the meadowlark; the smell of the land as it bakes under the sun."
—from the prairie website www.visi.com

At one time, elk, buffalo, wolves, black bears, and deer grazed on the tall prairie grass. Then, as more and more land was used for farming, those animals had to move to other areas to survive.

Today, animals such as the prairie chicken, prairie dog, snapping turtle, toad, badger, gopher, red fox, deer mouse, coyote, cottontail rabbit, and white-tailed deer live on the prairie. Birds such as the hawk and meadowlark also make their homes there. Even insects such as the butterfly and carrion beetle live on the prairie.

Hundreds of types of plants grow naturally on the prairie. The four most common prairie grasses in Illinois are:

• Big Bluestem   • Indian Grass   • Little Bluestem   • Switch Grass

Farms and growing cities took over much of the prairie. Today, most of the original prairie is gone.

MOVEMENT:
People, Products, Ideas, and Information Move

People travel from place to place, sharing their ideas and trading their goods. Early people traveled great distances. They traded ideas and tools with other groups. This made them better hunters, fishermen, craftsmen, and farmers.

Today, people from countries all over the world move in and out of Illinois. Some stay for a short time, to do business or take a vacation. Others come here to live. Movement of goods and information links Illinois with all parts of the world. Our location in the middle of the country means that people and things are always moving through our state. Shipping goods on our rivers is a big business. We sell livestock, field crops such as soybeans and corn, processed foods (foods made and packed in factories), minerals, and other things to places all around the world.

In our modern world, the Internet is an example of how ideas and information move. A young girl in Japan can learn all about Illinois while sitting at her computer. A young boy in Illinois can learn about Japan while sitting at his computer. They can send information back and forth to each other, or to any part of the world.

RELATIONSHIPS:
How Do People Use and Change the Land?

All through history people have *adapted* to and changed the environment around them. People have always cut down trees and grasses and gathered rocks and earth to build homes. They built their homes near a river or lake. Some groups planted gardens. They hunted wild animals and fished the streams. They gathered nuts and berries. They used the land to meet their needs.

We still use wood for homes today. We also use bricks, which are made of clay from the earth. Much of our food still comes from plants grown in the ground. We have found ways to take oil, coal, and other minerals from the ground. People also build roads, bridges, and dams. They plant new varieties of plants. People change the environment when cars and factories put chemicals into the air.

Major Rivers

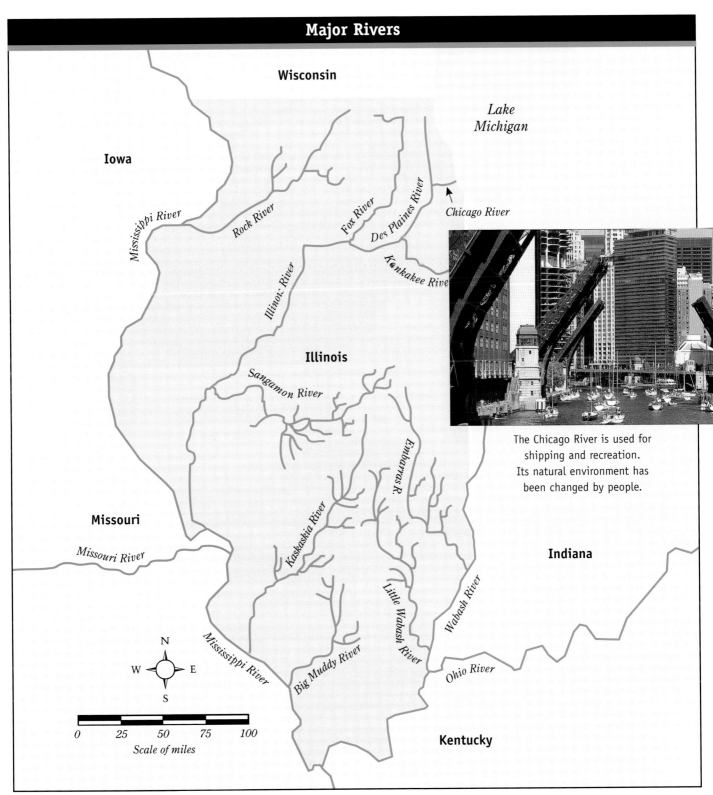

Wisconsin

Lake Michigan

Iowa

Mississippi River

Rock River

Fox River

Des Plaines River

Chicago River

Illinois River

Kankakee River

Illinois

Sangamon River

The Chicago River is used for shipping and recreation. Its natural environment has been changed by people.

Embarras R.

Missouri

Missouri River

Kaskaskia River

Indiana

Little Wabash River

Wabash River

N
W   E
S

Big Muddy River

Ohio River

Mississippi River

0   25   50   75   100
Scale of miles

Kentucky

▶ Photo by Karen L. Hirsch

People fish in our many rivers. Rivers add interest and beauty to the land. Rivers are also very important for transportation. We have built canals to link rivers together. We use our river system to ship goods to and from cities and countries around the world.

COAL

MILLIONS OF YEARS AGO, THE LAND WAS A SWAMP WITH LARGE PLANTS. WHEN THE PLANTS DIED, THEY WERE SLOWLY COVERED BY LAYERS OF SAND AND MUD.

PRESSURE AND HEAT FROM THE LAYERS TURNED THE PLANTS INTO COAL.

MINERS DUG THE COAL FROM ITS "BED." THEN THEY COVERED THE MINE WITH SOIL AND PLANTED SEEDS SO NEW PLANTS WOULD GROW.

WE USE SOME OF THE COAL RIGHT HERE BUT . . .

MUCH OF IT IS MOVED BY TRAIN, TRUCK, OR SHIP TO PLACES AROUND THE WORLD.

MOST OF THE COAL IS USED TO MAKE ELECTRICITY. THE COAL IS CLEANED BEFORE IT IS BURNED SO IT WON'T POLLUTE THE AIR AS MUCH.

COAL WILL CONTINUE TO BE AN IMPORTANT SOURCE OF ENERGY IN THE FUTURE.

Land of Many Natural Resources

The coal under almost two-thirds of Illinois has been very important to the growth of industry in our state. People built factories where there was plenty of coal for fuel and rivers for transportation. Later, railroads and highways made shipping coal and goods easier.

In addition to coal, oil and limestone are found in Illinois. At one time iron and lead were mined in the area around Galena. There are *fluorite* deposits in southern Illinois. Throughout the state sand and gravel are taken from the land and used in construction. We call these minerals natural resources. They are things found in nature that people can use. Plants, animals, and waterways are also natural resources.

The Ice Age

Illinois' land did not always look like it does today. How did it get to be this way? To answer this we must go back millions of years. Long ago Illinois was covered by a shallow sea called the Silurian Sea. We know that the sea existed because small sea creatures formed coral reefs under the sea. Those coral reefs are found underground today.

Millions of years passed and the earth changed. The sea dried up, leaving behind warm swampy lowland. Many kinds of trees and plants grew in the area that used to be covered by the sea. Over time the swampy lowland began to look like a tropical forest. The warm moist climate was perfect for amphibians and reptiles. No people lived anywhere on the entire earth's surface at that time.

More time passed, and the earth changed again. The climate became colder. As the climate got colder, the lush tropical forest died. The creatures that lived in the tropical climate had to adapt to the cold, move to a warmer climate, or die.

Year after year the climate grew colder. Summers were cool enough that the snow from winter didn't melt. It piled up winter after winter. No one really knows why the climate changed.

Glaciers Shaped the Land

As the snow piled up it became so heavy that the top snow pressed the bottom snow into sheets of ice. These huge sheets of ice are called glaciers. Some glaciers were more than a mile high.

The glaciers became so heavy that they started to move very slowly. They moved like giant blankets of ice scraping over the land.

Ice Age Glaciers in Illinois

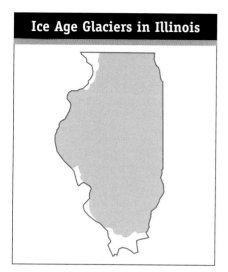

The shaded area was covered by glaciers.

Sand, gravel, medium-sized rocks, and boulders as big as a house stuck in the glaciers as they pushed over the land. The *scouring* movement flattened the land underneath. As glaciers dropped off sand, rocks, and boulders, they filled in the central region of Illinois. It became a flat fertile prairie that was a perfect place for plants and grasses to grow.

For thousands of years the ice sheets spread south. Then the weather got warmer. The southern part of the glaciers melted and left behind hills of soil and rocks. Grass grew where the ice had been. But again and again the cold returned, bringing the glaciers.

At least four times during the Ice Age, glaciers spread across most of Illinois. One glacier, the Illinoisan, was the largest. It covered most of what is now the state of Illinois.

Ice Age Animals

The land closest to the glaciers was called the tundra. It was a flat land with strong winds. Only low-growing plants could survive in the cold windy climate. There were no trees on the tundra.

Even though the tundra was cold, it was home to animals such as the woolly mammoth and Jefferson's mammoth. We know that the Jefferson's mammoth lived in Illinois because *fossils* have been found in DuPage and Pope Counties. Mastodons, deer, giant sloths, bison, saber-toothed cats, beavers as large as bears are today, and other animals also roamed Illinois during the Ice Age.

The mammoth was the largest Ice Age animal.

The saber-toothed cat hunted the ground sloth.
These animals are now extinct.

Glaciers Melted, Forming Lakes and Rivers

Finally, about 10,000 to 15,000 years ago, the climate of the earth began to warm up. The glaciers began to melt and break apart. As the ice melted, rivers began to form and flow into lakes. The Great Lakes were formed as a result of melting glaciers. Melting glaciers also formed the Mississippi River.

▶ Photo by John D. Ivanko

Lake Michigan was formed as a result of melting glaciers.

Taking Care of the Land

Illinois' land is always changing. Some change is very slow. Erosion and wind slowly wear away rock and soil. Natural events such as mud slides and tornadoes happen fast. Sometimes when there is a lot of rain the rivers and streams flood out over the land.

People also change the land. They build cities and freeways. They dig ditches, cut down trees, and build campgrounds. They plant new trees. They build bridges and make reservoirs. They dig into the ground to get coal and oil. These things can be important for people. They provide homes, food, fuel, and jobs.

If people and industries are not careful, though, they can harm the environment. There was a time when people often did not take care of the land. They thought people could never use up all the grass, trees, animals, and other resources. They thought there would always be plenty of fresh air and clean water.

Eventually, people began to think about using natural resources wisely. They passed laws to make it illegal for people or factories to pollute the air and water. They set aside some land for state parks and wildlife refuges. Today, most people are working together to keep our state a good place to live.

You Can Help

It is up to everyone to help *conserve* natural resources and protect the environment. Even you can help. You can stop littering. You can recycle cans and paper. You can turn off lights and televisions when you aren't using them. Everyone can help prevent forest fires caused by humans. Everyone can be careful to take care of Illinois.

activity

Reading a Map

There are many kinds of maps. Can you think of some? Perhaps you first thought of treasure maps. Or maybe you thought of the road maps your parents use on trips. Have you ever been to an amusement park and needed to find a certain ride? You probably located it on a park map. Look on your classroom wall for a fire escape map. It shows the best way to get out of the building during a fire. Maps help us get where we want to go.

Compass Rose   Most maps show the directions north, south, east, and west. You'll find these directions on a symbol called a **compass rose**. Find the compass rose on the map on the next page.

Legend or Key   Map makers use **symbols** so they don't have to write words all over the map. Whenever there are symbols, there is a **key** or **legend** that explains what the symbols mean. What do the symbols on this legend represent?

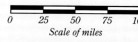

Scale of Miles   To show us how far apart things are, map makers use a **scale of miles**. This helps us measure the distance between places. Look on the map on the next page. How many miles are between Springfield and Chicago? Which is the shorter distance: Rockford to St. Louis, or Peoria to Milwaukee?

activity

Natural and Man-Made Boundaries

When the government divided our country into territories and states, it used imaginary lines as boundaries. These are the **man-made boundaries** that you see on maps. Sometimes natural features such as rivers form **natural boundaries**.

What kinds of things make up Illinois' boundaries? Other states? Bodies of water? Study the map on the next page and answer the questions.

1. How many other states border Illinois?

2. What body of water forms our western boundary?

3. What body of water forms our northeastern boundary?

4. What other bodies of water border Illinois?

5. Which of Illinois' boundaries are not bodies of water? (These are made by people, not nature.)

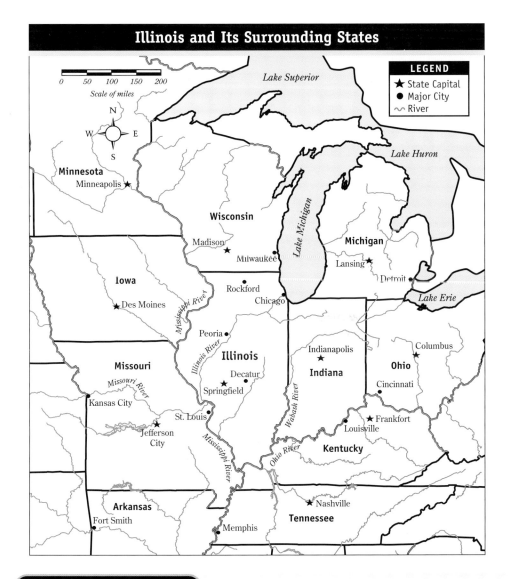

Illinois and Its Surrounding States

LEGEND
★ State Capital
● Major City
~ River

Scale of miles
0   50   100   150   200

Lake Superior

Lake Huron

Lake Michigan

Lake Erie

Minnesota
Minneapolis ★

Wisconsin
Madison ★
Milwaukee ●

Michigan
Lansing ★
Detroit ●

Iowa
Des Moines ★

Rockford
Chicago

Peoria ●

Illinois

Indianapolis ★

Columbus

Ohio
Cincinnati

Missouri
Decatur
Springfield ★

Indiana

Kansas City
St. Louis
Jefferson City

Mississippi River
Illinois River
Missouri River
Wabash River

Louisville
Frankfort ★

Kentucky

Ohio River

Arkansas
Fort Smith

Nashville ★

Memphis

Tennessee

Questions for Review

1. List the five themes of geography.

2. Describe why tornadoes happen in our state.

3. List four animals that live in our state.

4. What is an ecosystem? Describe the five natural ecosystems found in Illinois.

5. How have people in the past used our rivers? How do people use them today?

6. List Illinois' four land regions.

7. List three natural resources found in Illinois.

8. How did the glaciers shape our land?

THE TIME
12,000 B.C. to A.D. 1800

PEOPLE TO KNOW
Illinois Indian Groups
  Paleo people
  Archaic people
  Hopewell
  Mississippian (Mound
    Builders)
  Illini
  Fox
  Sauk
  Kickapoo
  Potawatomi

PLACES TO LOCATE
Gulf of Mexico
Appalachian Mountains
Lake Superior
Rocky Mountains
Collinsville
New York
Fox River
Wabash River
Lake Michigan
Starved Rock State Park
Illinois River

The First People

timeline of events

12,000 B.C.
Paleo people live all over North
America. They are the first people
in the Illinois region.

| 12,000 B.C. | 10,000 B.C. | 8000 B.C. | | 200 B.C. | B.C. 0 A.D. |

8000 B.C.
Archaic people live
a more advanced
lifestyle.

chapter

2

TERMS TO UNDERSTAND
artifact
archaeologist
mica
flint
community
thatch
alliance
wigwam
sapling
sap
shaman
legend
protective
clan
traditional

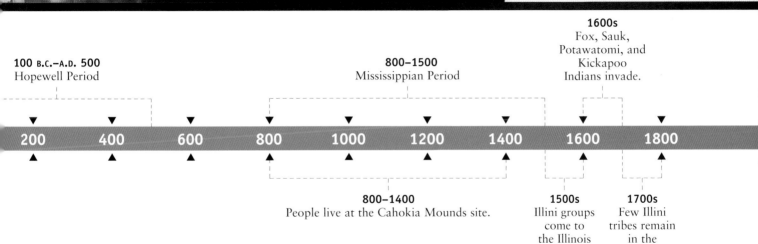

100 B.C.–A.D. 500
Hopewell Period

800–1500
Mississippian Period

1600s
Fox, Sauk,
Potawatomi, and
Kickapoo
Indians invade.

| 200 | 400 | 600 | 800 | 1000 | 1200 | 1400 | 1600 | 1800 |

800–1400
People live at the Cahokia Mounds site.

1500s
Illini groups
come to
the Illinois
region.

1700s
Few Illini
tribes remain
in the
region.

Ancient Indians

The first people who came to what we now call Illinois were probably following herds of wild animals. They hunted the animals for food. They must have been pleased with what they found. It was a land of quiet prairies and gentle streams. There were hills, woods, plains, and high bluffs. Mastodons and bison roamed the land. The rich soil left behind by glaciers made Illinois a good home. Plants grew very well.

The earliest people moved from place to place, following animal herds.

Paleo Indians

The earliest people were the Paleo people. "Paleo" means ancient. The people hunted animals and gathered food from wild plants. Later, they learned to store the food they had gathered in summer and fall. Then they did not have to move to find food in the winter.

Archaic Indians

The Archaic people were more advanced than the Paleo people. They developed better stone tools, such as knives, scrapers, and fish hooks. They developed a tool called an atlatl (ATL atl). The atlatl helped them throw a spear farther and with greater force.

They hunted animals and gathered nuts, fruits, berries, and seeds. They saved food in storage pits for the winter. They started to collect shellfish from the rivers for food.

An Archaic hunter uses an atlatl to throw his spear faster and farther.

Archaeologists

The people who lived here long ago left no written records about their lives. However, they did leave behind clues that tell us how they lived. They left *artifacts*, burial sites, rock art, and trash piles. *Archaeologists* examine these clues to learn how the people lived.

Archaeologists have learned that two periods of time were especially important. They are the Hopewell and Mississippian Periods. During these times, people made important changes in the way they lived.

Photo by David Blanchette

Archaeologists are scientists who study the things people of the past left behind. They must dig slowly and carefully. They try not to break tiny bones or artifacts that will help them learn about the people. Sometimes only a small brush is gentle enough to remove the dirt.

The Hopewell Period

Unlike others before them, the Hopewell people had enough food to stay in one place all year. They built rectangular houses in groups near the rivers. Most of their food came from wild plants and animals, but they also planted a few crops. They stored the food for the winter.

Living in one place made the Hopewell people different from those who had to move from place to place to find food. For example, the Hopewell took special care in the way they buried their dead. They formed large hills over the graves of their loved ones. Each hill contained many graves. Before, when people had moved around all the time, they had to bury their dead along the way.

Women wove cloth skirts to wear. They made loincloths for the men.

This drawing shows how a mound was made over the graves.

The Hopewell people traded with people in faraway places. Archaeologists have found shells from the Gulf of Mexico that were used for jewelry. They have found *mica* and copper. Mica is found near the Appalachian Mountains. The copper probably came from the land around Lake Superior. The people traded for new supplies to make tools, weapons, and jewelry.

The Hopewell people were probably the first to use money. They chipped pieces of *flint* into round, flat shapes. This money made trading easier.

The Mississippian Period

Another important time period was the Mississippian Period. The Mississippians came after the Hopewell people. They lived in the valleys along the Mississippi River. Like the Hopewell people, they built huge mounds, or hills. The Mississippians built the largest mounds. That is why we call them the Mound Builders.

The shape of each mound meant something to the people. They built them in the shapes of cones, pyramids, and animals. Sometimes they shaped the earth into birds, snakes, lizards, or even people. The mounds are also called earthworks.

The mounds had different uses. Many of the mounds covered graves. Often, the people built religious buildings on top of the mounds. Other mounds were used as forts. Some of the mounds were so large they looked like natural hills. However, we know by their shapes that these hills were formed by people.

The people hunted and fished for food. They searched the rivers for freshwater mussels and steamed them over the fire. They also gathered wild rice, seeds, and nuts. Mississippian farmers grew corn, beans, and squash. Corn became their most important crop.

Like the Hopewell people, the Mississippians traded with other Indian groups. They used materials brought from many faraway places. Scientists believe they traveled all the way from the Gulf of Mexico to Lake Superior, and from the Appalachian Mountains to the Rocky Mountains, trading with other Indians.

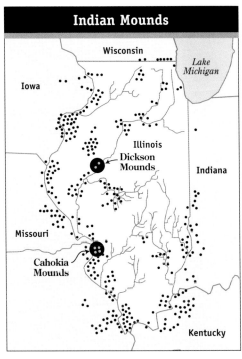

Indian Mounds

The two most famous mound sites in Illinois are Dickson and Cahokia. Each dot on the map shows other mound sites. Notice that the people built mounds along the rivers. They needed the rivers for water and for transportation. Do you live near any of the mounds?

The people ground the corn into meal.

Cahokia Mounds

The largest early *community* of Mound Builders was near Collinsville. Over 100 mounds have been found there. Experts believe that 10,000–20,000 Mississippian people lived there during its peak.

Most of the mounds at this site were rectangular and had flat tops. The people built important buildings on the tops for the leaders to live in. They also held ceremonies there. Other mounds were shaped like cones, but they were less common. They were built to mark important locations and to bury important people and their servants.

At one time there was a strong log wall around the center of the city. The wall protected the people from attack. It also helped to keep the wealthy people separate from the workers.

Some of the people lived in smaller villages and on small farms. These farms and villages were spread around the larger city.

Monks Mound

Monks Mound is at the center of the ancient city. It is so big that it was not built all at once, but in stages. Archaeologists believe a huge building once stood on the top of Monks Mound. The leader lived and ruled there.

Monks Mound was named in modern times after a group of monks lived there. Monks are men who have devoted their lives to religious activity.

We do not know what became of the Mound Builders. Their great city was left silent. The people may have used up all the local resources. Or perhaps changes in the climate hurt their crops and animals. Disease and poor nutrition could have ended their way of life. Or the whole group could have moved to another place. Maybe it was a combination of these things. For one reason or another, the Mound Builders disappeared from our land.

Monks Mound today.

▲ Photo by Tom Till

This statue was found near the ancient city.

*This is an artist's version of the Cahokia Mounds. Most people lived in a home they built using wooden poles for the frame. They used prairie grass to make a **thatch** roof. Can you see these homes in the distance?*

Illini Indians

After the Mound Builders disappeared, a group of tribes calling themselves *Illini* or *Illiniwek* moved into the region to live. Their name meant "the men" or "the people" in their language.

About twelve tribes made up the Illini group. Among them were the Kaskaskia, Cahokia, Peoria, Tamaroa (tam ah ROW ah), and Michigamea (mih shi GAH mee ah) tribes. They all spoke similar languages. The tribes agreed to share their hunting grounds, follow certain rules, and help protect one another. They believed that by joining together each tribe would benefit. This agreement is called an *alliance*.

The Illini people made their homes in the prairies and woods of Illinois. The way they lived depended on where they lived.

Northern Illini Groups

In the north, people depended more on wild foods than on farming. There were many plants, seeds, and nuts to be found. These tribes moved around often.

In summer, northern Indians lived in large groups near rivers and lakes. The men fished and the women grew small gardens. Near the end of summer the women gathered their yearly harvest of wild rice and vegetables. Soon afterwards, the families prepared to move. Each family took apart its *wigwam* and rolled up the birchbark cover.

During the winter, each family lived alone or with one or two other families. They moved from place to place, hunting buffalo or deer. They walked or traveled in birchbark canoes. The women carried the rolls of bark to rebuild their homes in each new place. The families were careful to stay within their own tribe's hunting grounds.

Everything the people used was made from what they found in nature. This canoe was made by hollowing out a tree trunk.

Southern Illini Groups

Farther south, farming was more important. Most Indians lived in year-round villages along the rivers. The villages were made up of long lodges. Like wigwams, the lodges had frames of bent *saplings*. The frames were covered with bark or mats made from reeds. Each lodge had a fire in the center and a hole in the roof for the smoke to escape.

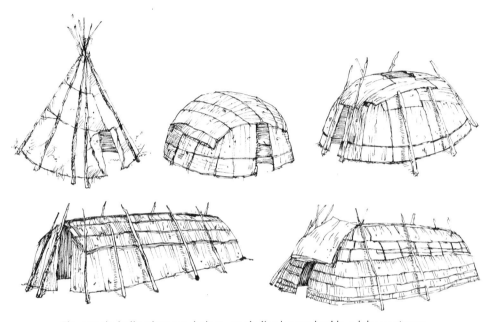

The people built wigwams, lodges, or similar homes beside a lake or stream.

Four or five families lived in each lodge. Some villages were large, with more than a hundred lodges. Like a row of apartments, each lodge was the home of several families. Inside, the people slept on beds built like shelves along the walls.

Outside the villages were fields. The women grew corn, beans, squash, and pumpkins. The men fished in nearby rivers and streams. In fall, some of the corn was dried, ground into meal, and stored in pits. Later, when there was more time, the corn would be made into a meal called hominy. Hominy, dried pumpkin, squash, and meat made up much of the winter food.

The people went on long deer and buffalo hunts. During hunting trips, tall wooden poles, stakes, and mats were carried and the women set up temporary shelters. As in the north, Indians who hunted outside the tribe's hunting grounds faced danger from other Indians.

In warm weather the people wore only a loincloth or skirt and deerskin moccasins. In the cold months they added robes and leggings made from animal skins to keep warm. On special occasions they wore jewelry, painted their bodies, and decorated their hair.

This man is storing his deer out of reach of wolves.

Linking the past to the present

Even today the place where we live has a lot to do with how we live. If you live in the northern part of the country, you have to dress warmly in winter, drive carefully in snow, and heat your house. If you live in the southern part of the country, you can wear shorts in the winter. Instead of heating your house, you try to keep it cool.

The Four Seasons

The people lived in harmony with the seasons.

Spring

Women collected **sap** from maple trees and planted seeds in the garden. Men and older boys fished. They used spears or bows and arrows to catch the fish.

Summer

The tribes left for the summer buffalo hunt. They went on foot or in canoes. In July they returned to the village to harvest corn and other crops.

Men and older boys hunted and fished. Women and children dried the meat and fish, cared for the crops, and gathered acorns, nuts, and wild fruit.

Fall

The tribes set out for another buffalo hunt. When they came upon a herd, the hunters made a circle around it. Then they started grass fires. This trapped the animals so they were easier to kill. The hunters used spears and bows and arrows to kill the animals. Women prepared the buffalo meat and dried the skins.

Winter

After the buffalo hunt the people returned to the village. They ate the food they had dried and stored.

Other Tribes Move In

Word of the rich hunting grounds in Illinois spread all the way to New York. The mighty Iroquois Indians lived there. Because European settlers were moving onto Iroquois lands, the Iroquois people decided to travel west to fight for the Illini lands. As they moved west they pushed the Sauk, Fox, Potawatomi (pot ah WAH toe mee), Kickapoo, and Miami tribes onto Illini lands. These tribes killed many of the Illini people.

As a result, the Illini split into smaller groups and moved in different directions. They became weaker and smaller.

Fox, Sauk, Kickapoo, and Potawatomi

The Fox Indians lived near the Fox River. They made traders and travelers who passed in canoes stop and pay a toll. After years of fighting other tribes in the area, the Fox people were almost wiped out. They joined the Sauk in order to survive.

An Englishman who explored the region described a Sauk village in his journal:

> This is the largest and best built Indian town I ever saw.
> It contains about ninety houses, each large enough for several families. These are built of . . . planks neatly joined, and covered with bark . . . to keep out the . . . rains. Before the doors are . . . comfortable sheds, in which the inhabitants [people] sit, when the weather will permit, and smoak their pipes.
>
> The land near the town is very good. In their plantations [gardens], which lie adjacent [next] to their houses, and which are neatly laid out, they raise . . . Indian corn, beans, melons, . . . so that this place is esteemed [thought to be] the best market for traders to furnish themselves with provisions [supplies], of any within eight hundred miles of it.

At one time the Potawatomi tribe took over much of Illinois, moving south to the Wabash River. Their lands stretched all around the lower part of Lake Michigan.

The Indian people met French and British explorers in the wilderness during this time. Often they took sides with the French or British when those countries fought each other. Later they would argue with new settlers over land.

Finally, the Fox and Sauk were forced out of Illinois by American soldiers. They settled west of the Mississippi River.

"The Iroquois approach like foxes, fight like lions, and fly away like birds."
—a Frenchman

The war paint, feathers, and earrings show that this Fox man is ready for war.

A Kickapoo man and woman do their chores.

Robes and hats made of fur kept
the people warm in winter.

Inside the wigwam life was warm and cozy.

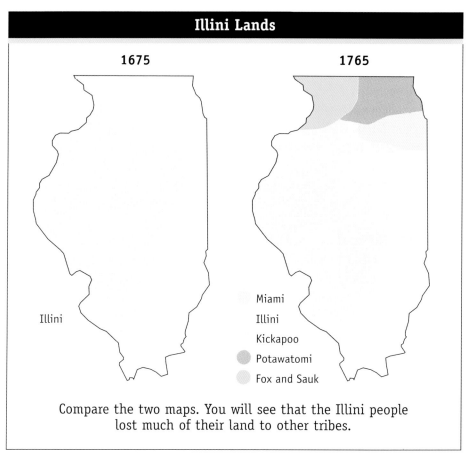

Illini Lands

1675   1765

Illini

Miami

Illini

Kickapoo

Potawatomi

Fox and Sauk

Compare the two maps. You will see that the Illini people
lost much of their land to other tribes.

Starved Rock State Park

Starved Rock

Along the Illinois River is Starved Rock State Park.
Inside the park is a high flat rock called Starved Rock.
The way Starved Rock got its name is an interesting
story.

Starved Rock
State Park

After the Illini alliance had lost much of its
power, a small group of Illini escaped to the top of
the rock. They knew they could defend themselves
easily from the enemy tribe below. The rock stood
high above the river and could only be reached from
one side. On the other three sides there was a drop of
more than 150 feet to the river below.

To get water, the people used long vines to lower their water
vessels to the Illinois River. But their plan did not work. Some of
their enemies hid near the base of the rock. They cut the vines each
time the Illini tried to get water from the river. After a while there was
no more food. One by one the Illini died from lack of water and food.
They chose to die rather than give themselves up to their enemies.

American Indian Lifestyles

Sharing the Work

The men and women of the tribe shared the work. The men hunted, built the wigwam, and made the weapons. They used wood and stone to make knives and bows and arrows. They made canoes out of tree trunks. Most tribes also made pottery for carrying water or food.

The women planted corn, beans, and squash. They also gathered food. They dried corn, berries, fish, and meat for the winter. If a woman had a baby, she carried it on her back on a cradleboard and went about her chores. In the winter she wrapped the baby in moss and fur and set it in the cradleboard.

The women also made animal furs into robes and warm clothes. They sewed animal hides into moccasins. They wove baskets, mats, and belts from strips of tree bark and plant fibers.

If you were an Illini child you were treated like a responsible member of the tribe. You helped fish and gather food. You worked in the garden. You learned important skills by watching adults.

This woman carries her baby on a cradleboard.

Games and Celebrations

There was a lot of work to do, but the people also played games. Girls played with dolls. They dressed them in the costume of their tribe. Boys practiced their aim with a bow and arrow. The games were fun and they helped to sharpen hunting skills. For example, in the hoop and pole game, the "hunter" tried to throw a pole through a moving hoop. This helped him to hit a moving target. They played lacrosse and held races and contests to test their speed and strength.

Music and dancing were important as well. The people danced to bring the deer or buffalo near and to get the corn to grow. They sang songs and played drums or rattles.

A Spiritual People

The people believed the world was full of spirits and special powers. The *shaman*, or medicine man, was the religious leader. The people held ceremonies to ask the spirits for help, to celebrate, and to have a good hunt or success in a war.

American Indians lived close to nature. They knew all about the land. The ground under their feet was more than just grass, rock, and dirt. The sun in the sky was more than just a ball of fire. They wanted to see and feel and touch the earth every day.

Sharing was important to most Indian people. Usually they said that all land that people farmed and hunted on and all rivers and lakes they fished in belonged to everyone in the group. They believed that the earth was made for the common good of people.

The shaman mixed plants and herbs to cure the sick.

Respect for Animals

American Indians shared the land with animals. They did not step on a snake's tracks or disturb the fox's den. Trees, flowers, squirrels, and insects all had the same value. They said the land belonged to the spider and the ant and the deer the same as it does to people. When they killed an animal for food they used every part of it. Nothing was wasted.

"I know I am a good person, and so are the things around me. Trees are good, birds are good, animals are good."

—Shirley Reed, an American Indian social worker

Legends and Myths

All of the tribes had *legends* that told their history. These were stories that explained how the tribe came to be. Legends also answered questions in nature, such as why the owl stays up at night or why the fox is so sly. They told of animals and spirits coming to teach or help the people.

Legends were told out loud from memory. They were passed from one generation to the next.

Why the Chipmunk Has Black Stripes

An Iroquois Legend

Long ago, the animals had tribes and chiefs just like the people. Porcupine was the chief of all the tribes because nothing could ever get close enough to hurt him.

One night, Porcupine called the animals together. He had a very important matter for them to consider. From tree tops and holes in the ground, the animals hurried in answer to the call.

They built a great blazing fire in the forest and seated themselves around it. Porcupine got up to speak. He looked very worried indeed.

"I cannot decide," he said, "whether we shall have night or daylight all the time."

That started a great argument. Some wanted it daytime always and some wanted it night. They all talked at once. You could not hear what anyone was saying, except Bear. He rumbled in a deep voice, "Always night! Always night! Always night!"

A little chipmunk became annoyed. Chipmunks hate to sit still for any amount of time. "You can talk all you like," he squeaked. "but the light will come whether you want it to or not."

The other animals went on roaring and growling. Chipmunk danced with excitement, shrieking, "The light will come! The light will come!"

Before they knew it, the sun rose above the tree tops. The fire looked weak and pale. It was daylight.

Silence settled upon the animals. Could it be possible that it was daylight whether they wished it or not?

A shrill voice suddenly came from the edge of the group. "What did I tell . . ."

"Grrrr!"

Chipmunk was gone like a flash through the trees with Bear after him. Bear was clumsy and Chipmunk was so quick that he slipped into a hole in a tree before Bear could catch him. But just before he disappeared, Bear struck at him with his paw.

The black stripes that run down the chipmunk's sides today show where Bear's claws hit him long ago when the animals tried to decide whether they should have darkness or daylight all the time.

These girls are dressed in jingle dresses. According to legend, the idea for the jingle dance came to a medicine man in his dreams. Women and girls perform the jingle dance.

The young boy on the left is wearing *traditional* Potawatomi clothing. The boy on the right is a grass dancer. His costume and dance recall the swaying movement of prairie grass on a windy day.

The Potawatomi Today

Esther Lowden is a Potawatomi woman. She answered these questions at a powwow in 1996.

Q: *How did the Potawatomi raise their children?*

A: Children were always taught that they were the future of the tribe. Parents were very **protective** of them. Just like in most of the tribes, the boys were taught to be the hunters and providers. They were trained to be the leaders.

The girls were taught to grow and prepare the food. They learned how to take care of the family. Girls were taught more about the medicines and the herbs used for healing. They helped the medicine man prepare herbs for different illnesses.

Q: *Were all members of the tribe trained the same way?*

A: The learning had a lot to do with the different *clans*. There were several different clans in the tribe, including the turtle, hawk, fox, deer, and bear. Whatever clan a child belonged to taught the child special skills. For instance, the turtle clan lived near the water. Children of this clan were taught skills relating to water, like fishing or making canoes.

Q: *What kinds of dances were performed by the Potawatomi?*

A: A lot of the dances were seasonal. There were harvest dances in the fall preparing for the winter. In the spring when the people planted seeds, and in the summer when they harvested food, they had other dances. Both men and women danced.

Q: *What was the most important crop for the tribe?*

A: Corn! They had several different ways they prepared it. There was dry corn in the wintertime. They made breads and soup out of it.

Q: *How do children today feel about tribal traditions?*

A: Most Indian children have a lot of respect for their traditions. There may be a few that don't want to participate, but most children learn it and remember. Even if they don't practice it now, eventually they will.

Q: *How many members are in the Potawatomi tribe today?*

A: There are over 20,000 members. If you can prove you have an ancestor who was a Potawatomi, you can become a member of the tribe.

Q: *What happens at your yearly powwow?*

A: The Potawatomi tribe puts on a three-day powwow each year. It is a contest. We give prize money and that draws many good dancers and drummers. People come from all over to see and participate in the event.

activity

Bury a Time Capsule

Would you like someone in the future to uncover things you've left behind? What could they learn about your lifestyle?

1. Collect a bunch of things that describe what your life is like now. Your class picture, a ticket stub from a sporting event or arts performance, and an empty box of your favorite cereal are all good things to put in a time capsule. Add pictures you've drawn of things you like (and don't like). You could even make a tape of your favorite songs.

2. Put everything into a waterproof container with a tight lid. Label the container with the date and the year you made it. Decorate it for fun.

3. Bury your time capsule in your yard for future people to find. What might they learn about you? Will their life be similar to yours?

Questions for Review

1. How did the first people in Illinois get food?

2. How were the Hopewell people different from those who came before them?

3. Why are people from the Mississippian Period called Mound Builders?

4. Which site has the largest mounds?

5. Why did the Illini Indians form an alliance?

6. What happened to the Illini Indians?

7. Name some of the crops the Indian people grew.

8. Why did the people tell legends?

Geography Tie-In

Give some examples of how the Indians used the land to meet their needs.

THE TIME
1670–1750

PEOPLE TO KNOW
Louis Jolliet
Father Marquette
La Salle
Henri de Tonti
Father Pinet
Philippe Renault

PLACES TO LOCATE
Europe
Great Britain
France
Spain
Canada
Atlantic Coast
St. Lawrence River
Mississippi River
the Great Lakes
Gulf of Mexico
Kaskaskia
West Indies
Galena River

Ruins at Fort de Chartres

timeline of events

1673
Marquette and Jolliet explore
the Mississippi River.

1675
Marquette starts a mission
near present-day Utica.

1696
Father Pinet
starts a
mission near
present-day
Chicago.

1670   1680   1690   170

1682
La Salle reaches the Gulf of Mexico and claims
the entire Mississippi River for France.
La Salle builds Fort St. Louis on Starved Rock.

1680
La Salle builds Fort Crevecoeur (krev KUR) near
present-day Peoria.

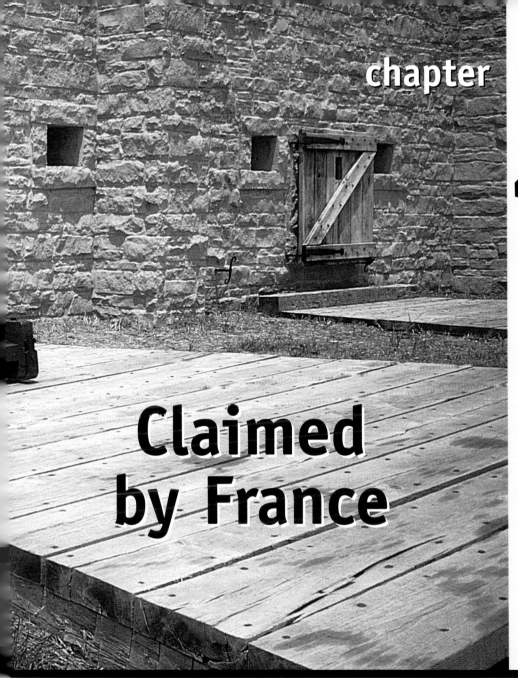

chapter

3

Claimed by France

TERMS TO UNDERSTAND
Jesuit
Christianity
mission
empire
colony
ambitious
barter
voyageur
rendezvous
portage
cargo
gentry
whitewash
surplus

1703
Kaskaskia
is settled.

St. Louis
Cahokia
Fort de
Chartres
Prairie
du Rocher

1719
Fort de Chartres is built near
present-day Prairie du Rocher.

1710   1720   1730   1740   1750

1699
The French set
up a permanent
settlement at
Cahokia.

1720
Black slaves are
brought to Illinois.

France Enters a New World

After Columbus visited North America in 1492, several European countries sent people to settle this land. Over two hundred years later, much of our continent was claimed by three countries—Great Britain (England), France, and Spain. European governments claimed the land, but hardly any European people lived here. Most of the land had not even been explored by white people. Except along the coasts, most of North America was inhabited only by American Indians.

Jolliet and Marquette

The land that we call Illinois was part of the French claim in North America. So were parts of Canada. The French governor in Canada sent Louis Jolliet (joh le ET) to find out where the Mississippi River led. Jolliet was an expert map maker. Father Jacques Marquette (mar KET), a *Jesuit* priest, was asked to go along. He had lived in Canada for seven years and had learned to speak many Indian languages. Marquette would teach the Indian people about *Christianity*.

Jolliet and Marquette paddled across Lake Michigan into Green Bay in two birchbark canoes. With the help of other boatmen, they followed Wisconsin rivers until they found the Mississippi River. They followed it south. When they were sure that the Mississippi flowed to the Gulf of Mexico, they turned back. They knew that if they kept going they would run into Spanish territory.

Marquette and Jolliet paddled back to Canada with exciting news. The soil was rich. The land was flat. Trees did not have to be cleared before houses could be built.

The Indians told the explorers of a great western river. We know this river as the Mississippi.

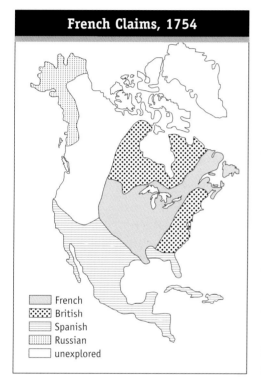

French Claims, 1754

French
British
Spanish
Russian
unexplored

The Indians had named the land *Illiniwek*, which meant "the men." The French changed the name to Illinois.

Louis Jolliet and Father Marquette were the first Europeans to travel the Upper Mississippi River. They traveled in birchbark canoes. How do we know about their journey? They kept journals and made maps.

Jolliet and Marquette's Route

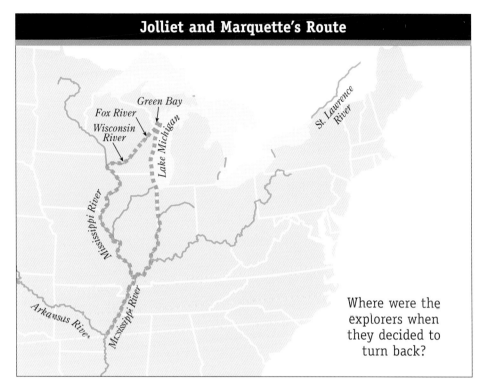

Where were the explorers when they decided to turn back?

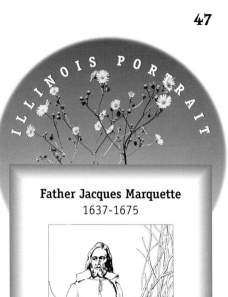

Father Jacques Marquette
1637-1675

Jacques Marquette was born in France. He was described as a gentle thoughtful boy. When he was seventeen years old he decided to become a priest. He wanted to become a missionary overseas. His wish came true when he was sent to Canada. There he studied Indian languages and started several missions. While teaching the Indians, he learned of a great river to the west. He also met Louis Jolliet. Marquette and Jolliet set out to explore the great river the Indians had spoken of. They were the first Europeans to see the Upper Mississippi River. (The Spanish had claimed the lower part.) Marquette traveled down the river, preaching to the Indian people along the way.

Jolliet and Marquette had visited American Indian villages near today's cities of Peoria and Ottawa. Father Marquette promised the Indians at a Kaskaskia village that he would return to teach them about Christianity. Later he did so and began the first *mission* in Illinois.

The French were interested in Illinois for another reason. They dreamed of a huge *empire* in North America. To have an empire, France knew it must stop its old rival, Great Britain, from becoming too powerful. Great Britain already had *colonies* along the Atlantic Coast. So France planned to control the middle of North America. Illinois was to be a part of that empire.

La Salle and Tonti

René-Robert Cavelier (kav uhl YAY), a wealthy Frenchman, had the title Sieur de La Salle. A *sieur* is a French knight or lord, so his title was similar to "Lord of La Salle." We call him La Salle for short.

La Salle was *ambitious*. Excited by the news of Marquette and Jolliet's trip, he made plans to develop the Illinois region. First he would start a fur trading company. He hoped that the Indians would trade only with the French. Then he would build a chain of forts from the St. Lawrence River to the mouth of the Mississippi River. (Find these rivers on the map above.)

The king of France was pleased. He gave La Salle land in Canada and put him in charge of the fur trade south of the Great Lakes.

**René-Robert Cavelier
Sieur de La Salle**
1643–1687

La Salle was born in Rouen, France. He studied to become a Jesuit priest, but then he left France and sailed to Canada. La Salle was given land near Montreal. He became a fur trader. He began to explore the land around the Great Lakes. He traded furs, built forts, and learned some American Indian languages. For a while he was put in charge of Fort Frontenac, but he wanted to explore farther west. La Salle and his partner, Henri de Tonti, set out to travel all the way down the Mississippi River. When they reached the Gulf of Mexico they claimed all of the land for France. They named the territory Louisiana.

During his travels La Salle met an Italian man named Henri de Tonti. Tonti had lost a hand in battle, so he wore an iron hook. La Salle and Tonti became partners. They led a group of men into Illinois. They built Fort Crevecoeur (krev KUR) near what is now Peoria.

La Salle wanted to be the first to travel down the Mississippi River all the way to the Gulf of Mexico. When he and his men finally reached the gulf, they held a ceremony. La Salle claimed the land on both sides of the river for France. He named it Louisiana, after King Louis of France.

Back the travelers went to Illinois. On top of Starved Rock, La Salle built Fort St. Louis. Then many Illini Indians built their homes near the fort for protection against other tribes. La Salle left Tonti in charge of Fort St. Louis. He returned once more to France.

La Salle traveled down the Mississippi River all the way to the Gulf of Mexico.
He claimed the whole river and the land next to it for France.

La Salle Runs into Trouble

La Salle had a new plan. He promised the king he would start a colony at the mouth of the Mississippi River. The king gave La Salle four ships and a crew of about 200 men. They left France for the Gulf of Mexico. But there was trouble right from the start.

One ship was captured by the Spanish. The other ships made it to the Gulf of Mexico, but they missed the mouth of the Mississippi River. Instead they landed on the coast of Texas. La Salle's crew was angry. The captain and some of the crew sailed back to France.

La Salle kept trying to reach the Mississippi River. Each time something tragic happened. The ships crashed and some men drowned. Finally the weary men had had enough. They shot and killed La Salle.

Tonti took over La Salle's work in the Illinois country. He built a larger Fort St. Louis near Lake Peoria. But he could not get many French people to make their homes in Illinois. It wasn't until Fort de Chartres was built that the French villages grew. The stone walls of Fort de Chartres made the settlers feel safer. The fort protected farmers, trappers, traders, and missionaries from unfriendly Indians.

Father Pinet

Pierre François Pinet (pee NAY) was a Jesuit priest. He set up a mission near present-day Chicago. It was called the Mission of the Guardian Angel.

Father Pinet hoped to teach the Indians in the area about Christianity and the Catholic religion. But the mission was not a success. It was abandoned after a few years. It would be about eighty more years before Chicago would become a permanent settlement. We will read more about the beginning of Chicago in a later chapter.

More French Follow

Soon other French people came to the Illinois region. Some were trappers who searched the rivers for beavers, so they could sell the furs in Europe. Others were priests, merchants, and farmers who set up more missions, trading posts, and small villages. The first two permanent European settlements were set up by the French at Cahokia and Kaskaskia. Other small villages, such as Prairie du Rocher, grew up around French forts.

The French changed the way the Indian people lived. The Indians no longer hunted animals only for their own food and clothes. Now they also hunted for furs to trade at the French trading posts. They traded the furs for goods such as metal knives, cloth, blankets, and sugar.

Near Utica, a group of Illini Indians prepared a feast for the men. When they saw Tonti's iron hand they thought he had special powers. La Salle and his men spent the night as the Indians' guests. Then they traveled on.

Henri de Tonti continued La Salle's work.

What do you think?

When the French came into the Illinois region they changed the Indians' lifestyle. Do you think the Indians changed the lifestyle of the Europeans?

The Mississippi River at Fort Kaskaskia.

Modern men are dressed as soldiers at Fort Massac. Find Fort Massac on the map.

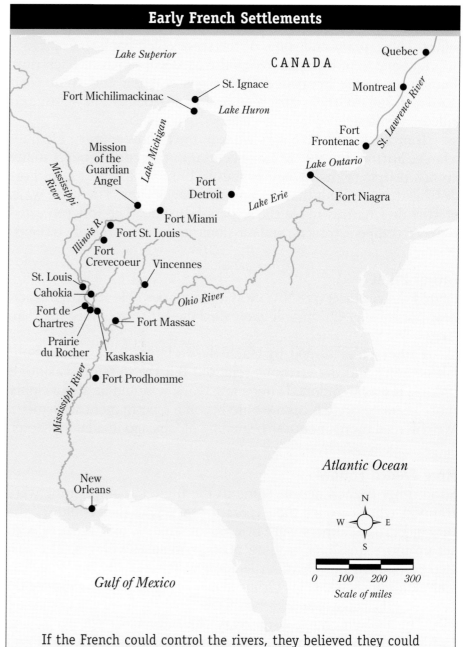

Early French Settlements

Lake Superior

CANADA

Quebec

Fort Michilimackinac

St. Ignace

Montreal

Lake Huron

St. Lawrence River

Fort Frontenac

Lake Ontario

Mississippi River

Mission of the Guardian Angel

Lake Michigan

Fort Detroit

Lake Erie

Fort Niagra

Illinois R.

Fort Miami

Fort St. Louis

Fort Crevecoeur

Vincennes

St. Louis

Cahokia

Ohio River

Fort de Chartres

Fort Massac

Prairie du Rocher

Kaskaskia

Mississippi River

Fort Prodhomme

Atlantic Ocean

N
W   E
S

New Orleans

Gulf of Mexico

0   100   200   300
Scale of miles

If the French could control the rivers, they believed they could control the region. They did this by building forts along the rivers. Find the fort that is farthest north. Find the one that is farthest south. Find Cahokia and Kaskaskia.

The Amazing Voyageurs

French merchants wanted furs they could sell in Europe. They wanted the soft thick furs of foxes, bears, otters, wolves, and beavers—especially beavers. Beavers were plentiful in Canada and the Illinois region.

Trading companies came to Canada to collect furs. At trading posts and forts, merchants and Indians **bartered** for furs. The traders offered a metal cooking pot for a tall stack of furs. When a fair trade was agreed upon, the items were exchanged. The furs were put into bundles that weighed ninety pounds. The bundles were then stored until a group of men arrived from cities in eastern Canada to carry the furs back to trading posts along the rivers. These men were called *voyageurs*.

A missionary who traveled often with the voyageurs described their way of dressing in his diary:

> *My man dressed himself in . . . a short shirt, a red woolen cap, a pair of deer skin leggings which reach from the ancles a little above the knees, and are held up by a string secured to a belt about the waist, the [cloth] of the Indians, and a pair of deer skin moccasins without stockings on the feet. The thighs are left bare . . . in winter and in summer.*

High Fashion

The beaver hat was the reason our land was explored so much by the trappers. For over 100 years, they were the fashion for European gentleman. Hat makers could hardly keep up with all the hats people wanted. People wanted fur for other reasons, too. It became popular for both ladies and gentlemen to wear fox, otter, and other animal fur on coat collars, sleeves, gloves, and boots.

The trappers in Europe had killed all the beavers there. When they learned that the land around Illinois had rivers full of beavers, they came here to trap them.

Fur trappers, traders, voyageurs, and Indians met at the **rendezvous** (RON day vu).
There they traded or sold their furs for things they needed, or for money. They also had
a great party. They ate, drank, had contests, told stories, and had a good time.

Modern men dressed as voyageurs paddle in a canoe race.

The job of the voyageurs was to paddle huge canoes filled with bundles of furs. The furs were going from the wilderness to large trading posts. Voyageurs could be found on rivers throughout Canada. They also worked on the Mississippi River and along the major rivers in Illinois. Voyageurs used the rivers of Illinois as highways for moving furs.

Often eight men spent fifteen hours a day paddling a canoe that was twenty to forty feet long and six feet wide. The canoes were so filled with furs that the paddlers could not change their kneeling position for much of the time they were paddling.

Sometimes the rivers or lakes the voyageurs wanted to use did not connect with one another. There was land in between that needed to be crossed. This land was called a *portage*. When it was time to move the canoes and furs over land, the men had to unpack everything from their canoe. Then they carried the *cargo* on their backs and shoulders. Somehow, they also had to carry the canoe. Some of the portages were five miles long. When the men reached the next body of water, they had to repack the canoe. To avoid making too many trips back and forth, the voyageurs carried more than one bundle of furs on their back. Sometimes they carried several at a time. Remember, each bundle weighed ninety pounds.

Linking the past and the present

Trappers and traders paddled the St. Lawrence River to different trading posts. Today, the St. Lawrence River is part of a major river system called the St. Lawrence Seaway. Ships of all kinds travel the seaway, bringing goods in and out of Illinois. The rivers are still important today.

Who Could Be a Voyageur?

Fur trading companies looked for special men to be voyageurs. First, they had to be strong. But they could not be too tall. Men with long legs could not kneel for long periods of time in the cramped canoes. Because of the heavy lifting and long hours of paddling, voyageurs developed strong muscles from the waist up.

The fur companies also looked for men with pride. Each voyageur felt he did something better than anyone else. It might be singing or telling stories about past trips. Some showed how strong they were by carrying more than one bundle on a portage. The men who paddled in the front and rear of the canoe took pride in their ability to miss rocks as they raced through rapids. All the men showed their pride by decorating themselves and their canoes with bright colors and feathers. A voyageur canoe could be quite a sight. Picture it in your mind: a brightly painted boat, feathers front and back, eight men singing at the tops of their lungs as they steer left and right to miss dangerous rocks in a roaring river.

Voyageurs spent months on rivers and lakes. To help pass the time they sang songs. Often the songs helped the men paddle faster or with the same rhythm. Mostly, their songs helped them through long hours of hard work.

Life in French Villages

French villages in Illinois were made up of small houses along narrow streets or paths. The houses were built close together for safety. A church stood at the center of most villages. The Roman Catholic religion was very important to the French villagers. Often the priest served as the schoolteacher for the children in the village.

Outside the village, each family had a long, narrow strip of land reaching to the riverbank. They made the fields long so they wouldn't have to turn their heavy plows too often. This also allowed every family access to the river. They used the river for water and transportation. Each village also had a large pasture where the cattle and horses grazed.

French Homes

The French settlers built one of two kinds of homes. If they were *gentry*, or upper class people, they built a stone house. If they were common people, called *habitants*, they built a home with a wooden frame. The walls were made of wooden strips. They filled the places between the strips with a mixture of straw and clay.

This drawing of a French home in Kaskaskia appeared in a French magazine in 1826. Would this home belong to the gentry or to *habitants*? Why do you think the home was built up on stilts?

Most houses had a single door, two or three windows, and a clay or log floor. A wide porch sometimes ran all the way around the house. The people **whitewashed** the houses many times, inside and out. All the houses had steep roofs. They were covered with straw or thin pieces of wood.

Inside, the house was divided into two rooms, usually with an attic. In one room was a fireplace for heating and cooking. The other room was a bedroom. A ladder led to the attic, where the children slept on feather beds or straw.

There were not many women in French Illinois. This meant that girls sometimes married in their early teens. Many French fur traders married Indian women.

French Food

The whole family helped with the farming. The people had learned from the Indians to grow corn, beans, squash, pumpkins, and melons. They ate these foods and fed them to their animals. The people also ate some meat—mostly pork or dried beef. They added to their meat supply by hunting and fishing.

Because the land was so good for farming, a family often had left-over crops to sell. This is called a **surplus**. Wheat, oats, and tobacco grew well in the rich soil. The surplus crops were sent to New Orleans along with bacon, buffalo hides, and furs. There they were sold or traded for sugar, rice, furniture, tools, and clothing.

The French at Work

Everyone was busy when there was planting or harvesting to do. Between those two seasons, the men went on hunting trips and trapped animals for the fur companies. They also traded with the Indians to get furs. Some men worked on boats going up and down the Mississippi River.

The women made the clothing for the family. They sewed red and blue cotton dresses for themselves and their daughters. They made blue shirts and pantaloons for the men and boys. They made deerskin moccasins for the whole family.

The villagers spent their money carefully. First came tools, then plenty of red and blue cotton cloth for the year's clothes. People with more money could buy coffee and maybe some silk or satin and lace for party dresses. Only the gentry had enough money to buy a piece of fine carved furniture.

The yearly arrival of goods from France was as exciting as any holiday. The whole village turned out when the boat came into sight. "Papa! Mama!" the children shouted. "Hurry! Hurry! It's coming!"

Butter was a special treat. It was made by beating or churning cream until it became stiff.

The settlers used copper kettles to cook soup and heat water over the fire.

The whole family rushed to the dock. It would be a full year before they would see so many tools, furniture, and fabrics again.

The French at Play

The villagers visited each other on Sundays after church. Everyone, young and old, sang folk songs and danced. They had many parties and feasts, especially on holidays.

Most of the time the French people got along well with the Illini Indians. Together they fished, hunted, trapped, and explored. Because of the missionaries, some Indians went to French churches.

American Indians and French settlers are both at this celebration in a French village near Kaskaskia.

African Slaves in Illinois, 1752

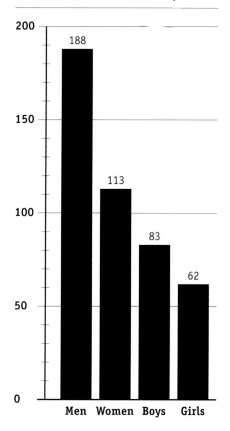

1. What year is shown on the graph?

2. Which was higher, the number of African men or women?

3. Were there more boys or more girls?

4. Why do you think there were more male slaves?

5. How many slaves were there in Illinois in 1752?

Slavery

In 1720 Philippe Renault (fil EEP ren OH) brought slaves to Illinois. Renault planned to open mines where there might be gold or other valuable minerals.

Renault stopped in the West Indies and bought black slaves on his way to Illinois. He planned to use the slaves for the hard work in his mines. He would also use them to farm his land and grow food for the miners.

Renault, his slaves, and other miners started to mine lead at the mouth of the Galena River. The demand for lead was great. It was used to make water pipes, tools, and bullets.

Before Renault returned to France, he sold his slaves to French villagers. For the next 100 years, some people in Illinois owned slaves.

Different Cultures Meet

People of different cultures met in the Illinois region. They had different lifestyles and beliefs about the land they shared. How did their lives affect each other?

American Indians   French settler   African slaves

activity

Weighing In
How much does this book weigh?
Use your math skills to figure out how
many books it would take to equal
ninety pounds. (That's how much a
bundle of furs weighed.) How many
books would you have to carry to
equal one bundle of furs carried by
the voyageurs? How much do you
weigh?

Suppose you were in charge of collect-
ing supplies for a trip with voyageurs.
On a piece of paper, list the supplies
you would put in their canoe. What
supplies might they carry on their
bodies?

Questions for Review

1. Which European country sent the first explorers to Illinois?

2. Which explorers found out where the Mississippi River led?

3. What did Jolliet and Marquette report about the land in Illinois?

4. Who was the first explorer to travel all the way down the Mississippi River?

5. Name the first two permanent villages set up by the French.

6. What qualities did a man have to have to be a voyageur?

7. Describe the two kinds of homes in a French village.

8. Why were slaves brought to Illinois?

Geography Tie-In

1. At the time, Canada was called New France. Can you explain why?

2. On a map, trace the route Marquette may have traveled from France to Canada.
   What ocean did he cross? Then trace his route from Canada down the Mississippi River.

THE TIME
1750-1790

PEOPLE TO KNOW
Chief Pontiac
George Rogers Clark
Governor Patrick Henry
Jean Baptiste Point
   du Sable

PLACES TO LOCATE
France
Great Britain
Quebec, Canada
Montreal, Canada
New Orleans
Appalachian Mountains
Georgia
Atlantic Ocean
the Great Lakes
Lake Erie
thirteen colonies
Kentucky
Virginia
Pacific Ocean
Vincennes, Indiana
Wabash River

timeline of events

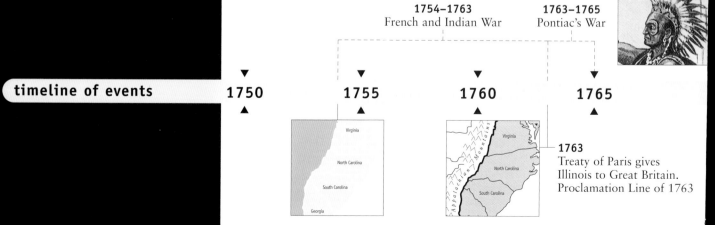

1754–1763
French and Indian War

1763–1765
Pontiac's War

1750   1755   1760   1765

1763
Treaty of Paris gives
Illinois to Great Britain.
Proclamation Line of 1763

chapter 4

Illinois Changes Hands

TERMS TO UNDERSTAND
rival
ally
proclaim
savage
custom
smallpox
independence
frontier
official
encourage
oversight

George Rogers Clark leads soldiers across the Wabash River.

1776 American colonies declare independence from Great Britain.

1778 George Rogers Clark takes Kaskaskia.

1779 Clark captures Vincennes. Illinois becomes a county of Virginia. Du Sable begins the first permanent settlement at Chicago.

1770	1775	1780	1785	1790

1776–1783
American War for
Independence

1784
Virginia turns
Illinois over
to the U.S.
government.

1787
Northwest Ordinance.
Northwest Territory
is created.

The French and Indian War

France and Great Britain were *rivals*. Each was trying to win a race. The race was for colonies and an empire. Both countries believed colonies would make them rich and powerful. The natural resources in the colonies would be used to make products for trade. The people living in the colonies would help build the empire. Countries were ready to go to war over their empires. And they often did.

France and Great Britain fought over colonies in the French and Indian War. It was the final contest to decide who was most powerful in the New World. French soldiers attacked the British forts and villages on the Canadian border. British soldiers attacked the French. Both sides got help from Indian *allies*.

For nine years the two countries fought. The war finally ended when the British captured the French cities of Quebec and Montreal in Canada. A peace treaty was signed. Great Britain got control of Canada and all the land east of the Mississippi River. The place called Illinois was now in British hands.

Many French people were not willing to live under British rule. Some left North America and went back to France. Some moved west of the Mississippi River or south to New Orleans. Other French people stayed, not knowing what would happen to them.

We call it the French and Indian War because the British fought the French and the Indians together.

Modern men dressed in costumes act out camp scenes from the French and Indian War.

Others also wondered about the future. American Indians had signed treaties about land. Britain and France had promised not to take Indian lands without permission. Now a peace treaty had been signed between the French and British. In the treaty, France gave Indian land to the British. But this was land the Indian people hunted on. It was land they used for their villages.

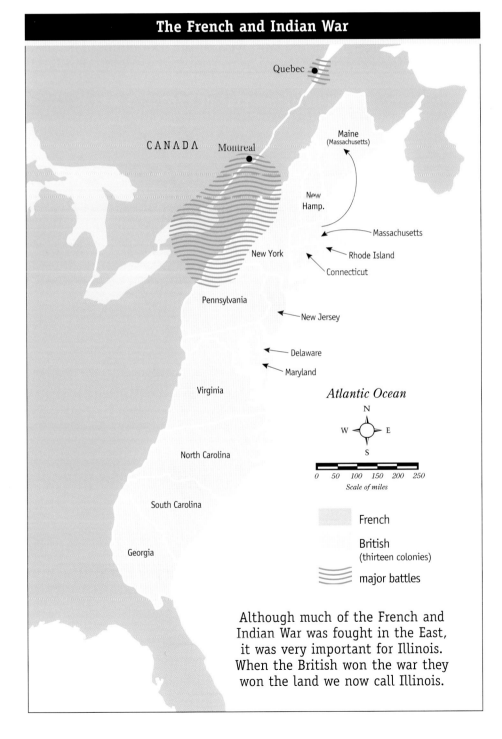

The French and Indian War

Although much of the French and Indian War was fought in the East, it was very important for Illinois. When the British won the war they won the land we now call Illinois.

The Proclamation Line of 1763

To settle the quarrels over Indian lands, the British government came up with a plan. It decided to draw an imaginary line down the Appalachian Mountains. The line went from Canada to the colony of Georgia. It was named the Proclamation Line of 1763. The government *proclaimed* that white settlers would not be allowed to cross the line going west. For the moment, Indian land was protected.

However, British colonists were bitter about the line. They had strong feelings about the land west of the mountains. They had just fought the French for the right to trap and settle on that land.

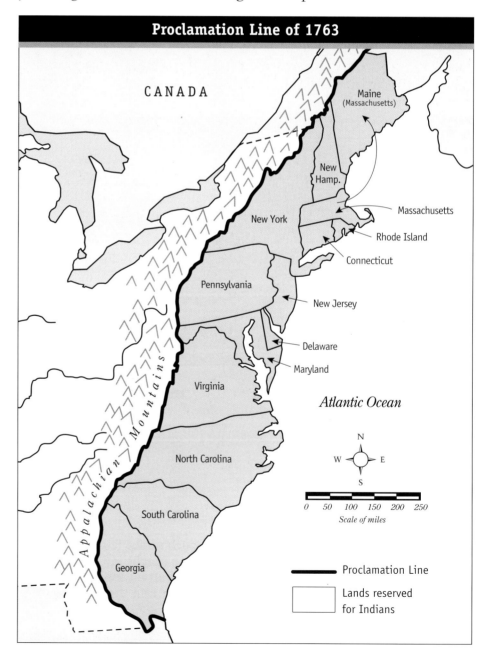

Proclamation Line of 1763

Many colonists thought of the Indian people as *savages*. They didn't think they deserved to have all of the land. Fur trappers and traders ignored the line and moved west onto Indian lands. Since the British government was all the way across the Atlantic Ocean in London, it couldn't do much to stop them.

Pontiac's War

A chief of the Ottawa tribe thought he had an answer. His name was Pontiac. He had heard stories about a prophet. The Indian prophet was wandering the wilderness carrying a map. He claimed the Great Spirit was angry with all Indians. He used the map to show the Indians how their land was disappearing. Pontiac believed the prophet and planned to take the Indians' land back.

As France and Great Britain signed their peace treaty, Indians met to talk about war. Men from tribes all around the Great Lakes gathered on the shores of Lake Erie.

At the meeting, Chief Pontiac stood up. He was tall. He was dressed as a warrior. He wore beads in his ear. Silver bracelets were on each arm. His face was covered with war paint. His black hair was cut short so his enemies could not easily grab it. He was ready for war.

Standing before the other chiefs, Pontiac spoke. He told them about the prophet and the words of the Great Spirit:

Chief Pontiac led a group of Indian tribes against the British.

> *I am the Maker of heaven and earth, the trees, lakes, rivers, and all things else. . . . The land on which you live I have made for you, and not for others. . . . My children, you have forgotten the* **customs** *and traditions of your forefathers. Why do you not clothe yourselves in skins, as they did, and use the bows and arrows, and the stone-pointed lances, which they used? You have bought guns, knives, kettles, and blankets from the white man, until you can no longer do without them; and what is worse, you have drunk the poison firewater [alcohol], which turns you into fools. Fling all these things away. And as for the English . . . wipe them from the face of the earth. . . .*

Pontiac's speech was a war cry. During the next few months, the fighting was terrible. The Indians destroyed all but four of the British forts near the Great Lakes. The British tried everything to stop Pontiac. They even sent blankets infected with **smallpox** to Indian villages. But the chief of the Ottawa people kept up his war.

After a while, the British got stronger. Pontiac's men began to leave him. Eventually, Pontiac could do no more. He signed a peace treaty. He was killed three years later by an Illini Indian.

The Great Lakes Region

Lake Superior

Lake Huron

Lake Michigan

Lake Ontario

Lake Erie

Illinois

Indian tribes living around the Great Lakes joined with Pontiac to fight for their land.

A young flutist at Fort Massac is dressed as he would have been during the War for Independence.

The War for Independence

Britain's thirteen colonies in North America declared their *independence* in 1776. They named themselves the United States of America. Of course, just saying they were free did not bring freedom. The new "Americans" had to fight a war to gain freedom from British rule.

▲ Photo by Karen I. Hirsch

 The War for Independence is also called the Revolutionary War. Look up the word "revolutionary" in the dictionary. Explain why the war was given that name.

The Declaration of Independence

Representatives from the thirteen colonies told the world they were a new country on July 4, 1776. In a paper called the Declaration of Independence, they explained why they broke away from Great Britain. One of the reasons was the Proclamation of 1763. Colonists wanted to move west. British soldiers had been sent to the colonies to stop them from crossing the mountains. The writers of the Declaration of Independence did not feel this was fair. They added it to their list of reasons for becoming their own country.

George Rogers Clark

Most of the fighting took place in the thirteen colonies. However, battles were also fought west of the Appalachian Mountains. One of them took place in Illinois because of George Rogers Clark.

Clark became worried about the British and their Indian friends. The British held forts at Kaskaskia in Illinois and Vincennes in Indiana. From these forts they could attack Americans in Kentucky, Clark's home, at any time. Britain's Indian allies were already raiding American settlements.

Clark Asks for Help

Clark asked for help from the governor of Virginia. Virginia had claimed Indiana and Illinois. But Governor Patrick Henry told Clark that no help would be coming. All his men and supplies were needed to fight the British in Virginia.

Clark was angry. He wrote a letter back to the governor. In it he said, ". . . If a country is not worth protecting, it is not worth claiming." Governor Henry thought about the problem again. This time he sent gunpowder to Clark. He also told him to form an army to protect Kentucky.

Clark could only get less than 200 men to join him. But the tiny army set out for the British forts just the same. The men left Louisville, Kentucky, by boat and floated down the Ohio River. About 100 miles from Kaskaskia they left their boats and went on foot. Six days later they could see the fort. The small army hid deep in the forest until dark.

By dawn, Clark's men had the town surrounded. When the people woke up they found their streets guarded by fierce-looking bearded men. They locked themselves in their cabins.

Clark saw a chance for victory without bloodshed. He went from cabin to cabin to talk to the people. He told them they came as friends. Slowly, people left their cabins to join the soldiers in the streets. By the end of the day, the people of Kaskaskia and the soldiers from Kentucky were celebrating together. Kaskaskia was no longer a threat to Kentucky and not a shot had been fired.

Clark and his men soon faced another danger. Almost half of his men had signed up to be in the army for only a few months. It was time for them to go home. After they left, Clark and the remaining soldiers were outnumbered by the Indian allies of the British. Clark decided to bluff his way to safety. He invited the Indians to a meeting. At the meeting he offered them a choice. They could pick war or peace. Impressed by his courage, they agreed to peace. Again, not a shot was fired.

ILLINOIS PORTRAIT

George Rogers Clark
1752–1818

George Rogers Clark did not have much schooling as a boy, but he went on to be a success. As a young man he worked as a surveyor, measuring the land. He lived in Kentucky, which was then part of Virginia.

During the War for Independence, Clark convinced the government to give him supplies to fight the British. He won for the United States the huge region where Illinois, Ohio, Michigan, Indiana, and Wisconsin are today. He also helped with the settlement of this new territory. He became friends with many Indians and French settlers. He returned to Kentucky near the end of his life.

". . . If a country is not worth protecting, it is not worth claiming."
—George Rogers Clark

The Job George Rogers Clark Turned Down

The new American government asked Clark to explore the land west of the Mississippi River. No American knew what was between the United States and the Pacific Ocean. But Clark refused.

Twenty years later, his younger brother William took the job. William Clark, along with Meriwether Lewis and forty-eight other men, traveled from St. Louis to the Pacific Ocean. Sacajawea, a young Indian woman, traveled with them as a guide. Lewis and Clark brought back many notes about the weather, plants, animals, and American Indians. Their travels helped open the West to settlers.

Clark was still worried. Surely the British at Vincennes would attack when the weather improved. Many of his soldiers were now gone. The remaining men would never be able to hold off a British attack. He would have to attack first. He would depend on surprise again. No one would expect him to march to Vincennes during the winter.

A Long March

Clark gathered about 200 men. Almost half of them were French settlers who had never been soldiers. In early February, the little army set out on foot toward Vincennes. The trip took almost three weeks. They waded through mud and water sometimes a foot or two deep, sometimes up to their necks. They had to be careful not to be seen by the enemy or unfriendly Indians. That meant camping with no fires to dry and warm them. Clark had to work day and night to keep up the men's spirits. With a week of marching left, they ran out of food. They went five days with only one deer to eat.

Finally the weary army reached Vincennes. They attacked the fort. The British were not prepared. They could not believe they had been attacked in the middle of winter. They turned the fort over to Clark the next afternoon.

By taking Vincennes, Clark won the Illinois region for the Americans.

Clark leads soldiers across the Wabash River.

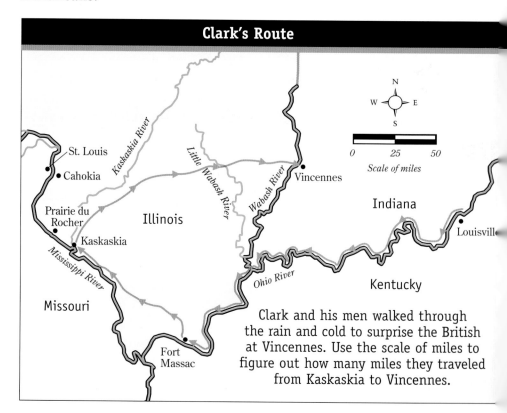

Clark's Route

Clark and his men walked through the rain and cold to surprise the British at Vincennes. Use the scale of miles to figure out how many miles they traveled from Kaskaskia to Vincennes.

Goodbye to British Rule

After seven years of fighting, Americans won their independence. They also won lands that doubled the size of the country. The new United States of America stretched all the way from the Atlantic Ocean to the Mississippi River. The Illinois region was part of the new country. But Illinois was not yet a state. The state of Virginia still claimed it owned the land called Illinois.

The Oldest Bell in the West

When Kaskaskia was first settled, King Louis of France sent the villagers a bell as a gift. Then the town was taken over by the British. Later, the people of Kaskaskia rang that bell in celebration when George Rogers Clark captured their town. They were happy they were no longer under the rule of the British soldiers.

Chicago is Born

Jean Baptiste Point du Sable, a black fur trader, set up the first permanent settlement at the mouth of the Chicago River. Du Sable's trading post became popular with Indians and trappers. With his wife he ran the trading post, farmed, and set up a mill. He also worked as a carpenter. Their home was more than just a log cabin. It contained mirrors and pictures, which were rare on the *frontier*.

Chicago, 1820

ILLINOIS PORTRAIT

Jean Baptiste Point du Sable
1745–1814

Jean du Sable was born in Haiti. His father was a French sea captain. His mother was an ex-slave. After going to France to be educated, he worked on his father's ship. He came to the Illinois region to trap furs. Du Sable married a Potawatomi Indian woman and they had two children. During the Revolutionary War he was captured by British soldiers. When he was set free, he moved to the north side of the Chicago River where it enters Lake Michigan. There he opened a trading post. Over time, Du Sable's trading post became the city of Chicago.

The Du Sable family lived there until 1800 when they sold the business and moved. Later they returned. Once again Du Sable set up his home and business there. He worked hard to make it a good place for trade and settlement. The small community around his trading post grew to become the city of Chicago.

Land of Stinky Onions?

What does the name "Chicago" mean? The answer is not clear. The name seems to have been the title for Indian chiefs in the region for a long time. Indians also called the river and swampy region at the tip of Lake Michigan *Checagou*. Another form of the Indian word, *Eschikagou*, meant the "place of bad smells." The odor of the swamp and its wild onions could have been the reason for the name.

The Northwest Territory

Virginia was finding it hard to govern a land so far away and so full of wilderness. Virginia gave the Illinois region to the U.S. government.

The U.S. government passed a plan for the new territory. The plan was called the Northwest Ordinance. (An ordinance is a rule or law.) Now that our region belonged to America, the government made it an **official** territory. They named it the Northwest Territory. It included the lands that would become the states of Ohio, Indiana, Illinois, Wisconsin, Michigan, and part of Minnesota.

Why was Illinois called the Northwest? Isn't the Northwest where states like Oregon and Washington are? Well, at the time, Illinois was about as far north and west as the settlements in our country stretched. To the people living then, it *was* the Northwest!

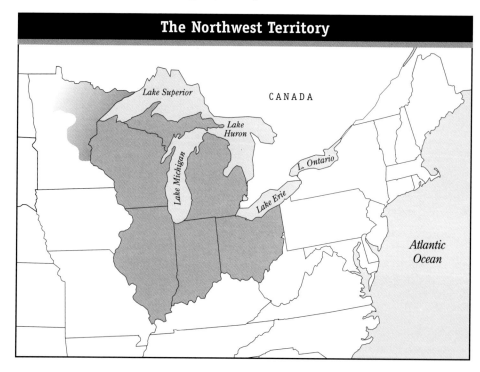

The Northwest Territory

The Northwest Ordinance

The Northwest Ordinance set rules for the Northwest Territory. The rules were supposed to *encourage* settlers to come and make the land their home. Here are some of the rules:

- Slavery would not be allowed.

- Education would be encouraged.

- Settlers would have the freedom to follow whatever religion they believed in.

- Settlers who came to the territory would have the right to a trial by jury.

The Northwest Ordinance had an eye toward the future. It set rough boundaries for how the territory could be broken up later into states. It also set rules for how those regions could become states.

The one important issue that the ordinance did not cover was American Indians. It ignored the Indians who had been on the land first. This *oversight* led to many problems.

Let's review how Illinois changed hands:

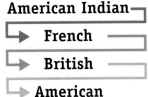

What do you think?

- If you were a settler, do you think the rules would encourage you to come or keep you away? Why?

- Why do you think the writers of the Northwest Ordinance ignored the Indians?

Questions for Review

1. Who fought against whom in the French and Indian War?

2. Why did the British government draw an imaginary line down the Appalachian Mountains? What was the line called?

3. What did Chief Pontiac do?

4. George Rogers Clark won the Illinois region for which country?

5. Who is the founder of Chicago?

6. Which future states did the Northwest Territory include?

Geography Tie-In

List the groups of people that moved in and out of the Illinois region during this time period.

THE TIME
1800-1840

PLACES TO LOCATE
Northwest Territory
Illinois Territory
Vincennes, Indiana
Canada
Chicago
Chicago River
Lake Michigan
Illinois & Michigan Canal
Kaskaskia
Vandalia
Springfield

PEOPLE TO KNOW
Ninian Edwards
Jean Baptiste du Sable
John Kinzie
Nathaniel Pope
Daniel Pope Cook
Shadrach Bond

Becoming a State

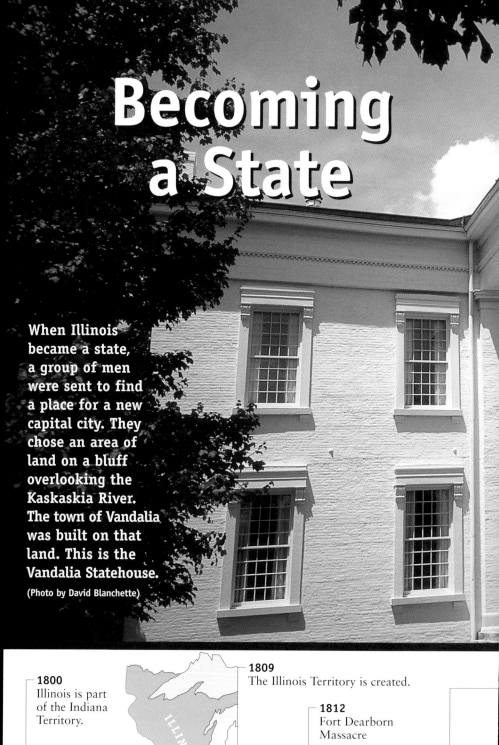

When Illinois became a state, a group of men were sent to find a place for a new capital city. They chose an area of land on a bluff overlooking the Kaskaskia River. The town of Vandalia was built on that land. This is the Vandalia Statehouse.

(Photo by David Blanchette)

timeline of events

1800
Illinois is part of the Indiana Territory.

1809
The Illinois Territory is created.

1812
Fort Dearborn Massacre

ILLINOIS TERRITORY

1800   1805   1810   1815

1803
Fort Dearborn is built.

1812–1815
The War of 1812 is fought with Great Britain.

1817
Illinois' first newspaper, *The Illinois Herald*, is published.

chapter 5

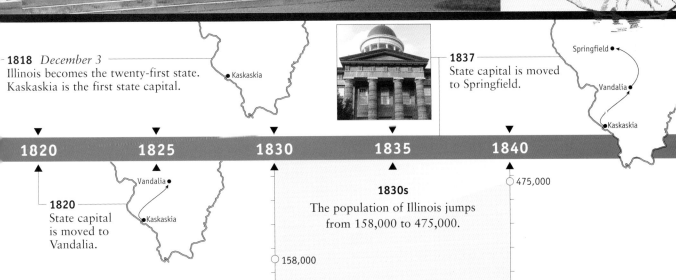

1818 *December 3*
Illinois becomes the twenty-first state.
Kaskaskia is the first state capital.

1837
State capital is moved
to Springfield.

1820   1825   1830   1835   1840

1820
State capital
is moved to
Vandalia.

1830s
The population of Illinois jumps
from 158,000 to 475,000.

475,000

158,000

The Illinois Territory

The Northwest Territory covered a large area of land. In fact, it was such a huge territory that it was difficult to control. The people living there felt they didn't have enough protection from angry Indians. They felt like they had been forgotten by the government.

To solve this problem, Congress divided the Northwest Territory into smaller pieces. Each smaller piece would have representatives and government leaders. One of the smaller pieces was the Indiana Territory. The new territory included the land that would become Illinois.

To the people living there, the Indiana Territory still seemed too big to be *efficient*. The government headquarters were in Vincennes. The settlers in Illinois complained that it was too far away to really help them. They didn't have enough protection or control over what happened to them, they claimed.

It took another nine years for Congress to organize the Illinois Territory. Ninian Edwards was chosen to be the territorial governor.

Illinois was one step closer to becoming a state, but it wasn't a state yet. For one thing, the Illinois Territory didn't look like Illinois does today. The northern border went all the way up to Canada. It included land that would become several states.

The town of Kaskaskia was chosen to be the capital of the new territory.

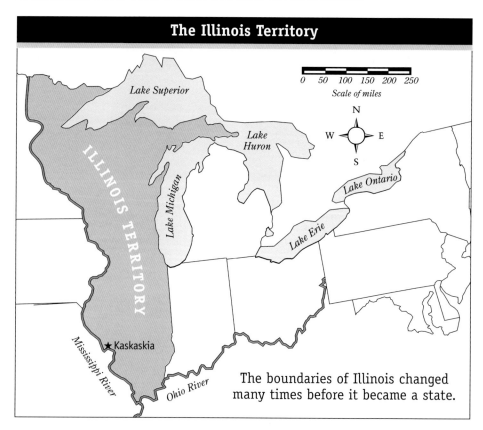

The Illinois Territory

The boundaries of Illinois changed many times before it became a state.

Fort Dearborn

In the last chapter you learned that Jean Baptiste Du Sable and his wife ran a trading post where Chicago is today. They collected furs from Indians in exchange for metal goods, wool blankets, and other items the Indians wanted.

Du Sable had to close his trading post during the Revolutionary War. He and his wife returned when the war ended. They stayed until 1800.

A few years later, the U.S. government built a fort where Du Sable's trading post had been. They built it to protect the people living at the mouth of the Chicago River. It was called Fort Dearborn.

Fort Dearborn was made of sturdy logs placed upright in the ground. There were two log walls around the fort. If anyone attacked the fort, they would have to climb over the first wall before they could reach the second. The only holes in the walls were high above the ground. Soldiers inside the fort stood on walkways near the tops of the walls and aimed their rifles through the holes.

Inside the fort were houses for sleeping and storing supplies. There was a well for fresh water. A tunnel ran from the fort to the shore of Lake Michigan. If the people inside ever needed to escape, they could sneak through the tunnel to the edge of the lake.

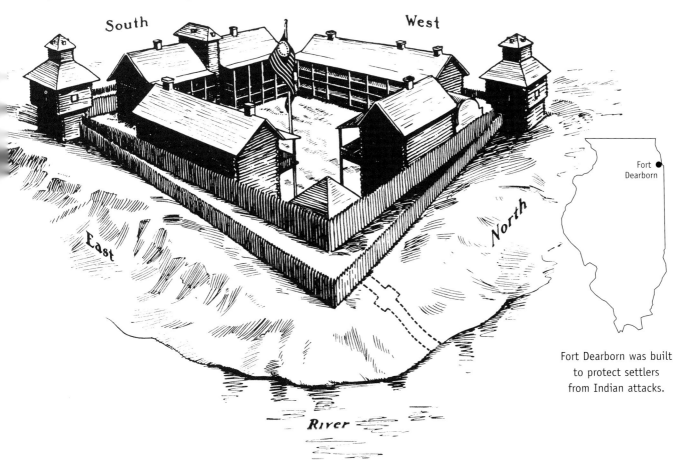

Fort Dearborn was built to protect settlers from Indian attacks.

Far right, photo by John Lynn

Treaties with Indian Tribes

Treaties were used to get land from Indian tribes. Often land was exchanged for money, tobacco, salt, or animals. Some exchanges included land in new locations. The following tribes made treaties with Illinois leaders.

Delaware
Miami
Potawatomi
Ottawa
Wea
Kickapoo
Kaskaskia
Sauk
Piankesh
Michigamea
Cahokia
Tamaroa
Chippewa
Fox
Peoria

Many believe that the people at Fort Dearborn would have been safe if they had stayed in the fort.

Indian Troubles and the War of 1812

The land in the Northwest Territory had been Indian land. But the Northwest Ordinance let Americans decide how the land would be used. The Indians thought this was unfair. They were not invited to the meetings to decide who should own the land.

Angry Indians attacked American settlements. They stole horses, tore down fences, and destroyed crops. Sometimes they killed settlers.

Meanwhile, the British still hoped to end America's dream of being independent. Another war between the United States and Great Britain began. This became known as the War of 1812. Some Indian groups helped the British fight the Americans. They wanted to drive the Americans off the land. Governor Edwards urged the government to do something to protect the settlers. He wrote,

No troops of any kind have yet arrived in this Territory, and I think you may count on hearing of a bloody stroke upon us very soon. . . .

The Fort Dearborn Massacre

After British soldiers had captured a nearby fort, the community at Fort Dearborn knew it was not safe from attack. On a hot day in August, the soldiers at Fort Dearborn got orders to leave. They were told to take the settlers living nearby to Fort Wayne in Indiana. But friendly Indians warned them not to go. There were not enough soldiers to make the trip safely, they said. They would have to travel past hundreds of unfriendly Indians camped on the shore of the lake.

John Kinzie and other settlers agreed. The trip to Fort Wayne would be too dangerous. They had enough food and guns to stay in the fort for months. But the fort's commander felt he had to obey his orders. They would go to Indiana.

On August 15, 1812, the soldiers and settlers marched out of the fort. *Fifes* and drums led the way. Before they had gone two miles they were attacked. A bloody battle followed. The Indians killed or captured almost everyone. John Kinzie, his family, and a few other settlers escaped with the help of friendly Indians. The next day the fort was burned. The bloody battle has become known as the Fort Dearborn *Massacre*.

The Fort Dearborn Massacre is remembered as one of the most horrible events during the settling of Illinois. Years would pass before pioneers dared to return to the area that would be Chicago.

The war with Great Britain ended in 1815. The British could not win back the land they had once ruled. With the end of the fighting, American settlers began to come to Illinois again.

It's hard to imagine that this is the place where pioneers were once afraid to settle.

All for a Piece of Illinois

Why did the British try once again to get land in America? Why was there so much fighting over this land? Part of the answer is that it is a land of many resources. Soil, minerals, waterways, and animals are all things people use. Illinois has all of these things.

Forty-One Miles Made All the Difference

Nathaniel Pope worked hard to make Illinois a state.

If you live in one of the following counties, take note! If Nathaniel Pope had not gotten our state boundary moved forty-one miles north, you would be living in Wisconsin today.

Jo Daviess
Carroll
Whiteside
Lee
Stephanson
Winnebago
DeKalb
Boone
Kane
Ogle
DuPage
Cook
McHenry
Lake

Those forty-one miles made all the difference because they included Chicago and its waterways. Without Chicago, Illinois would be a different state with a different history.

Statehood

As the number of people in Illinois grew, so did their interest in becoming a state. Why did everyone want Illinois to become a state? What was wrong with being a territory?

Territories were allowed to send **delegates** to Congress to represent the people. The delegate for the Illinois Territory was Nathaniel Pope. But there was a big problem. Nathaniel Pope could not vote in Congress. He didn't even have a say in the decisions Congress made about his territory. That was because Illinois was not a state.

If Illinois were a state, its people would have a say—a vote—in what happened to them and to other states as well. Another reason it was important to become a state was because states attracted more settlers. People wanted to settle in areas that were a part of the growing United States.

A young man named Daniel Pope Cook believed it was important for Illinois to become a state. He was Nathaniel Pope's nephew. He owned part of the territory's first newspaper, *The Illinois Herald*. He wrote articles in the paper telling people why Illinois should become a state. He urged a group of representatives from the Illinois Territory to ask for statehood.

Nathaniel Pope Asks for a Change

One of the first things Nathaniel Pope did was ask Congress for a new northern boundary for our state. Congress had proposed a boundary that was forty-one miles south of where it is today. Pope argued that this border would not do, because those forty-one miles included the shoreline of Lake Michigan. Illinois needed Lake Michigan for trade with states in the East. Without the shoreline for docks and warehouses, Illinois could only trade by slower land routes.

Pope had another reason to worry about trade. If Illinois could not trade with eastern states, it would have to get most of its goods from southern states. The goods would enter Illinois by traveling up the Mississippi and Ohio Rivers. But something else might come along with the goods—slaves. Pope did not want Illinois to become a state full of slave owners. Pope's request for a new border was granted.

There was an important **requirement** that a territory had to meet in order to become a state. It had to have a population of 60,000. In 1818, the Illinois Territory had only 40,000 people. But Nathaniel Pope and Daniel Pope Cook **negotiated** with Congress. Even though the Illinois Territory didn't have enough people, Congress agreed to let it become a state.

Now the Illinois leaders had to write a state **constitution**. If Congress approved the constitution, Illinois would be made a state.

The Delegates Meet

In July of 1818, thirty-three delegates from around Illinois met in Kaskaskia. Their job was to write a constitution for the new state. The men were elected by the people of Illinois. They were store keepers, ministers, doctors, lawyers, sheriffs, and flatboat workers.

The constitution was short and simple, and the men approved most of it pretty easily. But there was one matter the delegates argued and argued about, and that was *slavery*.

The Question of Slavery

Slavery is one person owning another person. The owner makes the slave work long hard hours for him without pay. When slaves were brought from Africa to America they were treated horribly. They were made to live in shacks. They were not allowed to learn how to read or write. Often they were beaten and whipped if they upset their owner, or "master." We will read more about the terrible practice of slavery in a later chapter.

Some of the delegates wanted slavery to be allowed in Illinois. Others did not.

The new state of Illinois did not allow slavery. Later, the General Assembly tried to make slavery legal, but they could not get enough votes. Illinois would stay a free state. Sadly, people still kept slaves and treated black people unfairly.

Illinois Firsts

FIRST NEWSPAPER:
The Illinois Herald

FIRST GOVERNOR:
Shadrach Bond

FIRST CAPITAL:
Kaskaskia

Do you know any other "Illinois Firsts"?

At the time, it was up to each state to decide if it would allow slavery. Most of the southern states did allow it. People in the South were mostly planters. They needed many fieldworkers to grow their huge crops of cotton, tobacco, rice, or sugar. They bought slaves to do this work.

The northern states did not allow slavery. Many northerners worked in other industries besides farming. There were farms, but they were smaller. In most cases, the families could do the work themselves. More and more people in the North believed that slavery was wrong. They wanted the slaves to have the same rights as everyone else.

Many of the delegates wanted to allow slavery in the new state of Illinois. They wanted slaves to work in the mines and fields. They said this would help Illinois compete with the eastern states. Others thought that slavery would take work away from poor white people. They also believed that slavery was *immoral*. They thought it was wrong to buy and sell human beings as if they were property. They wanted Illinois to be a free state.

Finally, those who were against slavery won. Even the men who wanted slavery agreed to outlaw it. They worried that Congress might reject their constitution if it allowed slavery. However, most of them believed they could still find ways to keep slavery around.

A State At Last

When the constitution was finished, the people of Illinois waited for Congress to act. On December 3, 1818, Illinois entered the United States as the twenty-first state.

Choosing a Leader

As soon as Illinois became a state its people were allowed to elect government leaders. They elected Shadrach Bond as the first governor. They elected senators and representatives to the General Assembly. The General Assembly made laws for the state. They met in Kaskaskia, Illinois' first state capital.

One of the first things the General Assembly did was start planning a *canal* between Lake Michigan and the Illinois River. The Illinois & Michigan Canal would let boats travel from Lake Michigan all the way to the Mississippi River.

The General Assembly also worked on the plan for a new state capital. The government hired *surveyors* to lay out a brand new town in Vandalia. In 1820 Vandalia became the state capital. By the end of the year a capitol building was built and the government moved in. Later, Springfield became the state capital.

The Capitals of Illinois

A new capitol building was built behind the old one in Springfield. This is the capitol building today.

This is the Old State Capitol in Springfield.

Springfield
1837

Vandalia
1820

Kaskaskia
1818

The capital was moved to Vandalia in 1820. Vandalia was the capital until 1837, when it was moved to Springfield.

Kaskaskia was Illinois' first capital city. This was the first capitol building.

ILLINOIS PORTRAIT

Shadrach Bond
1773–1832

Shadrach Bond came to Illinois from Maryland when he was twenty-one years old. He taught himself how to be a successful farmer. His warm personality and honesty made him very popular around his home in Kaskaskia. During the War of 1812, Bond was a captain in the U.S. Army. Later, when Illinois became a territory, he was chosen to be the first representative to Congress. When Illinois became a state, people voted for their governor. Bond was so popular that no one even ran against him.

activity

Reading a Graph

Graphs help us to "see" information. If you can read a graph you can learn the facts quickly.

It is always important to understand just what kind of information a graph is showing. The title and categories are good clues to the kind of information a graph contains. Study the graph. On a separate piece of paper, write down which of the statements below are shown as information in the graph.

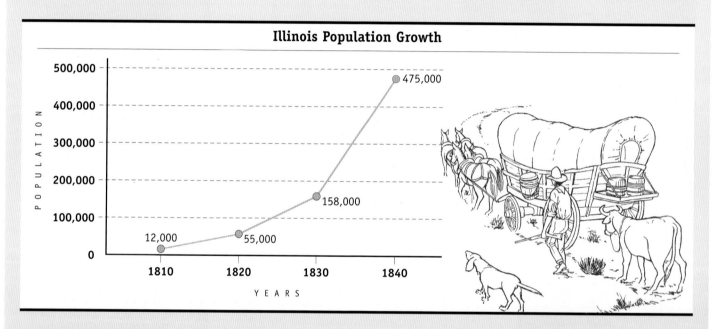

Illinois Population Growth

1. At first, pioneers mostly settled in the southern part of the state.

2. Between 1810 and 1820 the population of Illinois grew by 43,000.

3. After Illinois became a state (in 1818), the population grew.

4. There were many more settlers than Indians in Illinois by 1860.

5. In 1850, the population of Illinois was less than one-fourth of the population of the United States.

6. The population of Illinois more than doubled from 1820 to 1830.

Questions for Review

1. Why were the soldiers at Fort Dearborn told to leave?

2. List five Indian tribes that made treaties with Illinois leaders.

3. Why did the people want Illinois to become a state?

4. How did Daniel Pope Cook help Illinois become a state?

5. Why did Nathaniel Pope ask to move the Illinois border to the north?

6. When the delegates met to write our state constitution, what did they argue about the most?

7. Did our state constitution allow slavery?

8. On what day, in what year, did Illinois become a state?

9. Who was the first governor of the state of Illinois?

10. Where is the state capital today? What other Illinois cities were once the capital city?

Geography Tie-In

Looking at a map, try to imagine the shape of Illinois as if the border were below Lake Michigan. Draw the shape on a piece of paper. As a class, discuss how the following things would be different if Illinois did not include that land.

- The land
- The population
- Trade and industry

THE TIME
1800-1840

PLACES TO LOCATE
Northwest Territory
southern states
eastern states
Europe
Atlantic Ocean
Massachusetts
Mississippi River
Iowa
Pittsburgh, Pennsylvania
Springfield

PEOPLE TO KNOW
Christiana Holmes Tillson
Chief Black Hawk

timeline of events

1800
Waves of pioneers
begin to move to
Illinois.

1812
Fort Dearborn
Massacre

1815
Workers
begin
building a
national
road.

1800   1805   1810   1815

chapter 6

The Journey to Illinois

1818
Illinois becomes a state.

1828
Pioneers establish McKendree College, the oldest in Illinois.

1829–1832
Black Hawk War

1837
State capital is moved to Springfield.

Springfield •
Vandalia •

| 1820 | 1825 | 1830 | 1835 | 1840 |

1820
State capital is moved from Kaskaskia to Vandalia.

Vandalia •
• Kaskaskia

1830s
Illinois farms become more and more productive.

Moving West

Pioneers had begun to move west even before the Revolutionary War. Some, like the men who fought with George Rogers Clark, came as far as Illinois. They told others about the beautiful rich land in southern Illinois. When the Northwest Territory was created, more pioneers came to settle here. Even more people came when Illinois became a state.

The first wave of settlers came from southern states. They settled in southern Illinois, where there were woods and hills like in their home states. They found plenty of trees to use to build log cabins. They stayed away from the prairie. They thought the prairie soil would not be good for crops because there were not many trees there.

The next wave of settlers came from eastern states. Since the land along the rivers in southern Illinois was taken, they began to settle on the land between the rivers. Some settled more and more to the north. They found out that the prairie had very rich soil indeed. Since there weren't many trees, they built homes out of prairie sod.

Pioneers also came from European countries. They had to cross the Atlantic Ocean on a ship. But that was just the beginning. They still had to make the trip to Illinois.

"The first thing after a settler arrived was to find a suitable location and to set about building a cabin. Our cabin was a [c]rude structure with one room. . . . Trees of [the same] size were selected and notched, as to bring them as near together as possible. The cracks were 'chinked' [filled in with mud] to keep the wind from whistling through."
—Jeanette Pigsley Mitchell

The Journey to Illinois

When people traveled across land they walked, rode horses, or came in covered wagons pulled by horses or oxen. The wagon wheels could be taken off and the wagon bed used as a boat. White canvas was stretched to cover the arched wooden bows over the wagon.

It provided some protection for the travelers inside, but not much. When it rained, the roof often leaked. Things inside got wet. It was cold in the winter and hot in the summer.

Since the family carried everything with them it was very crowded inside. There were trunks, wooden boxes, furniture, oil lamps, bags of grain, a spinning wheel, and a butter churn.

The ride was very uncomfortable. People were jolted and tossed about from one side of the wagon to the other. Most of the time they walked beside their wagons.

> **After traveling all that way through trees and woods, the pioneers came out into the wide flat prairie. It was like nothing they had ever seen before.**

Westward, Ho!

In 1800, a poet named Moore wrote about traveling in a wagon:

> *Dear George, though every bone is aching*
> *   After the shaking*
> *I've had this week over ruts and ridges,*
> *   And bridges*
> *Made a few uneasy planks,*
> *   In open ranks,*
> *Over rivers of mud whose names alone*
> *Would make knock the knees of the stoutest man.*

Many families moved west to Illinois in wagons like this one.

Dirt Roads and Mountains

Early roads were only dirt trails and smashed-down grass. Most were old Indian trails. They were rocky and bumpy. Often there were large holes in the way. They got very muddy when it rained.

Travel was very slow. Sometimes a road was so narrow the wagons could not pass through the trees. Travelers had to stop, get out of the wagon, and chop down trees before moving on. This could take hours. Sometimes a horse's hoof or a wagon wheel got stuck in the mud.

Pioneers faced another problem—mountains. Pushing and pulling heavy wagons over slippery mountain rocks was scary. Sometimes the horses were frightened and would not go down steep canyons. Sometimes wagons tipped over. Mary E. Ackley wrote in her journal about crossing the mountains:

> *A dozen yoke of oxen were hitched to one wagon, and with hard pulling they reached the top. After all the wagons were over, we took lunch on top of the mountains, and then prepared to go down . . . the mountain was very steep. One yoke of oxen was hitched to a wagon, and one at a time went down. Heavy chains were fastened on behind the wagon and as many men as could catch hold of the chain did so, and when the wagon started*

What kinds of things do you think the people left behind?

An old pioneer road

Photo by John Lynn

they pulled back to keep the wagon from running down the mountain and killing the oxen. We were . . . exhausted . . . when we camped that night . . . for we had to walk all the way.

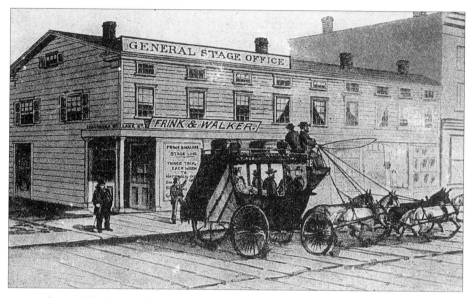

For a while the people tried covering the dirt roads with wide wooden planks. Notice the planked road in this picture.

Flatboats and Keelboats

Whenever they could, the pioneers used the rivers as highways. Going by boat was easier than going across land. They floated ***downstream*** on flat-bottomed boats called flatboats. They were hard to steer, and sometimes they turned over in rough waters. When families arrived, they broke their flatboats apart and used the wood to build other things.

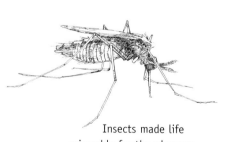

Insects made life miserable for the pioneers.

People and products moved on flatboats and keelboats between Illinois and many other places.

Keelboats moved upstream, against the river's *current*. They had to be rowed or pushed with long poles. Sometimes a rope was tied to the front of the boat. Then a crew of strong men or mules pulled the boat from the shore.

The men were known for their rowdy behavior. They filled the streets with their shouts and hollers:

I'm a ring-tailed roarer
and a ring-tailed screamer too!
I was raised on grizzly bear milk
and cradled with a wildcat.
I'm half horse and half alligator
and people call me the Mississippi Snag.
I can eat a dozen rattlesnakes for breakfast
and drink a barrel a' whiskey besides.
I can outrun, out-hop, out-jump and out-fight
any man in this whole country!
Ya-hooooooo! Yip-eeeeeee!
Stand back and gimme room!

Water Routes to Illinois

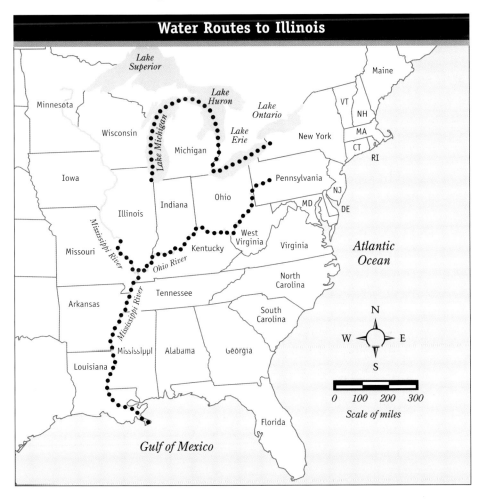

Pioneer Life

Imagine a life with no electricity, no plumbing, and no stores. That is what the settlers who first came to Illinois faced. Pretend you and your family have come to make a new life for yourselves. You would probably settle in the southern part of Illinois. That's where most families settled in the early years. Going farther north meant risking attacks by unfriendly Indians.

Getting Settled

First you find a good clear stream. It's important to build your house near water. You will need water for drinking, cooking, and cleaning.

You pick a spot near trees because you need wood to built your house, furniture, and fences. You also need the trees for firewood. You'll keep a fire burning almost all the time for cooking, heating the cabin, and warming water for your weekly baths.

Without a good strong house you won't be safe in the wilderness. You clear the land of bushes, grasses, and trees. If you're like most settlers, you build a log cabin. Father and the boys in the family cut down trees and build your cabin.

Once the cabin is up you build a stone fireplace. It is one of the most important parts of your new house. It is where Mother and the girls will do the cooking. It is also where the family will gather when it gets cold—and it will get cold.

No plumbing in your cabin means no running water. You must carry water in from the stream or from a well, if you dig one. Of course, no running water means no toilet. So the next thing you build is an *outhouse*.

A New Life

There is so much to do. There's land to clear and crops to plant and tend to. There's furniture to make. Just about everything you use has to be made by hand.

The girls help Mother sew and wash the clothes. You wash the clothes in the river by beating them with a club or hitting them against a rock. Or you might carry water to a large tub outdoors, heat the water over the fire, and wash the clothes there. It is hard and tiring work.

The boys help Father clear the land for farming. Chopping down trees and pulling up stumps is difficult. You are exhausted, but you still need to hunt and fish for food.

At night everyone goes to bed early. The only light is from the fireplace and from oil lamps. But you don't mind because you are so tired from all the hard work.

This statue in Vandalia honors pioneer women.

Photo by John Lynn

"Father had six girls, and only one boy, and much depended on us girls in assisting to clear his land and carry on his farming. Father was a farmer, teacher and preacher, and also did the shoemaking for the family. We girls helped to improve the old homestead and did much of the outdoor work."

—Jeanette Pigsley Mitchell

A Woman on the Trail

Christiana Holmes Tillson was one of many women who made the journey west to Illinois. She was from a well-to-do family in Massachusetts. Her story tells of the new life she started in the West.

In 1822 it was still a great event to undertake a journey to Illinois, and many were the . . . remarks and conclusions about my going. . . .

We had been traveling in a northwesterly direction . . . in order to head the water courses, there being no bridges in those days. . . . We came to the Kaskaskia River, where there was a rope ferry. I had never seen anything like it before. . . .

. . . we set our faces northward again, and soon after starting came to a large prairie; . . . This was my first introduction to a real prairie, and I must say I was sorely disappointed. . . . Father had talked so much about their beauty that I expected to feel a kind of **enchantment**. He said, 'you never saw anything like this before.' I said 'no;' but did not say I never saw anything more **dismal** . . . the autumnal fires have passed over, leaving them in all their blackness, with an occasional strip of coarse grass or a scrubby bush.

Pioneer children went to school about three months out of the year. The rest of the time they were too busy helping on the farm or doing other chores at home.

Pioneer Schools

As more and more pioneers moved into an area, they built a one-room schoolhouse. The outside of the school was usually made of logs. Inside, the floor was sometimes just dirt. Children sat on long wooden benches. There was no heating except for a stove that burned coal and wood. The children took turns bringing in wood to burn.

All the grades learned together in one room. Brothers and sisters sat in class together. The teachers were paid a little money and they got free room and board. This meant that the families with children at the school took turns having the teacher stay with them. They provided a bed and meals.

This one-room schoolhouse is very different from our schools today. Would you like to be in the same class as your brothers and sisters?

Learning and Discipline

Students learned their ABCs from the Bible or from a hornbook. A hornbook was a wooden paddle with letters and sentences written on it. Children wrote with chalk on small blackboards made of rock, called slates. Paper was very rare. Sometimes, for practice, children wrote on tree bark.

Learning meant memorizing. The teacher read a lesson to the students. Then the class repeated it over and over and over. One by one, the students stood up and *recited* the lesson from memory. If the child missed a word, or did not stand perfectly still while reciting, he had to do it over again until he got it just right.

Pioneer schools were strict. Students had to sit up straight, be quiet, and always have their lesson ready. Students who misbehaved or did not pay attention had to stand in a corner or were switched with a thin rod. Another common punishment was writing the same sentence hundreds of times.

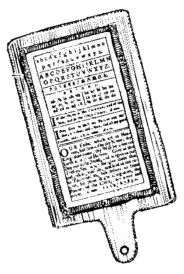

Students read such lessons as
F – the *Idle* Fool is Whipt at School.
Y – While Youth do Cheer,
Death may be Near.

What do you think?

Some people today like the idea of the one-room schoolhouse. They want to return to schools where different grades share the same classroom. They say learning is easier when the older children can help the younger ones.

Do you think school would be better with mixed grades? Or do you think it would be harder to learn that way?

The Black Hawk War

Pioneers were settling farther and farther north in Illinois. They were moving onto the fertile lands where Sauk and Fox Indians lived. Settlers were beginning to take over Indian fields and homes.

Sauk and Fox Indians had made a treaty with the U.S. government. They gave their land east of the Mississippi River to the government. They moved west to Iowa. But the agreement didn't last.

One of the chiefs, Black Hawk, said the treaty was not *valid*. He claimed the Indians were given alcohol to make them drunk so they would give up the land. He said the settlers should be the ones to leave. Black Hawk led warriors and their families back onto the land in Illinois.

Thousands of volunteer soldiers set out after the Indians. After days of tracking, the soldiers found them on the shore of the Mississippi River. The tired hungry Indians tried to cross to safety.

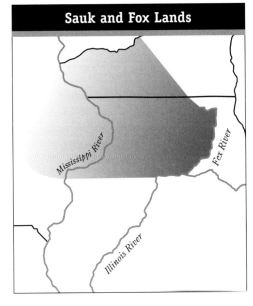

Sauk and Fox Lands

Mississippi River

Fox River

Illinois River

Black Hawk
1767–1838

Black Hawk was a brave chief of the Sauk Indians. He was born in a Sauk village near the Rock River. He fought with the British in the War of 1812. Black Hawk became angry about a treaty the Sauk and Fox tribes had signed with the U.S. government. He gathered warriors together and led them in a fight for their land. When the fighting was over, Black Hawk was forced to surrender. After the war he and the other Indians were forced to live on a *reservation* in Iowa. He wrote down his story, *The Autobiography of Black Hawk*.

They were no match for the soldiers. Hundreds of Indians died in the battle or drowned trying to cross the river. Those who did cross were attacked by rival tribes on the other side. Nearly the whole group was wiped out in just two days. Chief Black Hawk was captured.

When the war was over, all Indian tribes were ordered out of Illinois. To the pioneers, it was a signal to move safely into northern Illinois. To the Indians, it was another broken promise over land.

Photo by John Lynn

Black Hawk stands tall and proud in this statue.

activity

Write a Letter to a Friend
Pretend you are making the journey from Pittsburgh, Pennsylvania, to Springfield, Illinois. Your best friend back in Pittsburgh is going to make the same trip soon. Write your friend a letter describing your journey. With the help of a map, explain the best way for your friend to get from Pittsburgh to Springfield.

activity

What Would You Do First?
Join with a group of classmates. Suppose you are just arriving from your long journey to Illinois. You have ridden and walked many miles to get here. Now it's time to make your home.

1. What will you have to do? Try to think of as many things as you can. Make a list. Put the most important things first, then the next, and so on.

2. Compare your list with the lists of other groups. Did your group forget anything?

3. Which group in your class has the best chance of starting a successful settlement?

Questions for Review

1. The first group of pioneers came to Illinois from which area of the country?
2. List some difficult things the pioneers had to deal with on their journey west.
3. List three things a pioneer had to do after arriving in Illinois.
4. How did students in pioneer schools learn their ABCs?
5. Black Hawk was the chief of which American Indian tribes?
6. Why did Black Hawk think the treaty with the government was unfair?

Geography Tie-In

1. What things in nature (weather, landforms, animals, plants) helped the pioneers? What things in nature made the trip even harder?
2. How did the people change the land once they got to Illinois?
3. Talk about some of the things that were moved here from other places (people, things, ideas).

THE TIME
1820-1870

PLACES TO LOCATE
Pennsylvania
Cairo
Grand Detour
Moline
England
Ireland
Sweden
Kankakee
New York
Nauvoo
Carthage
Galena
Utah
Bishop Hill
Meredosia
Switzerland
Arthur
Arcola

PEOPLE TO KNOW
Robert Fulton
Cyrus McCormick
John Deere
Joseph Smith
Eric Jansson
Nicholas Ridgely
Jakob Ammon

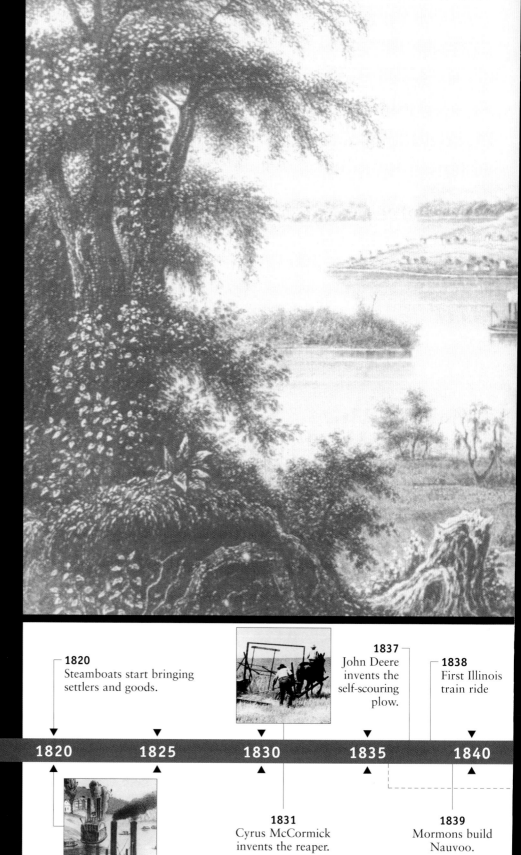

timeline of events

1820
Steamboats start bringing settlers and goods.

1831
Cyrus McCormick invents the reaper.

1837
John Deere invents the self-scouring plow.

1838
First Illinois train ride

1839
Mormons build Nauvoo.

1820   1825   1830   1835   1840

chapter 7

Settling Illinois

TERMS TO UNDERSTAND
ground
obstacle
manufacture
brawny
luxurious
scour
immigrant
convert
debate
legislature
speculator
crude
lock
locomotive
progress

1846
Bishop Hill is settled.

1850
Illinois is the fastest growing
state in the country.

1865
Amish families settle in
central Illinois.

| 1845 | 1850 | 1855 | 1860 | 1865 | 1870 |

1836–1848
Illinois & Michigan Canal
is built.

1852–1858
Illinois Central Railroad
is built.

Steamboats Change Travel

A man from Pennsylvania named Robert Fulton designed the first steamboat. His new kind of boat used a steam engine that had been invented in Europe. Wood and coal were burned to heat a huge container of water. When the water boiled it gave off steam. The steam pushed against parts of the engine, which turned huge paddles at the back of the boat. As the paddles turned the boat moved. This new kind of engine greatly changed travel and business. Steamboats could bring more people and supplies to communities along Illinois rivers.

Steamboats could move much faster than keelboats. Because they had flat bottoms, the water only had to be four feet deep for them to travel. This meant that they could serve hard-to-reach settlements. Their powerful engines helped them battle strong currents, carry heavy cargo, and tow barges.

Steamboat travel also had its problems. Big rivers like the Ohio and Mississippi were often filled with floodwater. When that happened, logs, sandbars, and some islands were hidden under water. Even experienced riverboat pilots *grounded* their boats or sank them by running into hidden *obstacles*. Sometimes the steam boilers exploded and fire swept through the boat. Steamboat crews also faced the danger of pirates along lonely stretches of river.

Steamboats delivered the mail and brought supplies to many river towns.

Cairo

Flatboats, keelboats, and steamboats are shown in this scene at Cairo. Can you find each kind of boat?

Visiting a Steamboat

Suppose you could visit a steamboat in 1845. You stand at the edge of a pier, waiting for the boat to come into sight. You hear its deep whistle in the distance. The pilot blows the whistle to let everyone know the boat is arriving. Everyone around you is getting ready to meet passengers or pick up cargo. They move their carts and wagons into position.

You hear another blast from the whistle. This one signals the crew to get ready for the landing. The engine must change speed to slow down.

Soon you can see smoke over the trees. The smoke is coming from two smokestacks rising high above the boat. The smoke is thick and black. It's coming from coal and wood being burned as fuel.

As the boat approaches, you see that it carries many passengers. It also has a deck full of *manufactured* and agricultural goods. You hear someone playing the calliope (cah LIE oh pee). This musical instrument is like an organ but it is powered by steam. The song is lively and the passengers are enjoying the music.

As the boat edges closer, ropes fly in the air. Ropes must be thrown to workers on the dock. Crew members shout to one another. Just above your head are the landing stages. These wooden ramps can be swung out from the boat when the steamboat stops at places that don't have docks. With the help of the stages people can easily walk to the shore.

> "Your true pilot cares nothing about anything on earth but the river, and his pride in his occupation [job] surpasses [goes beyond] the pride of kings."
> —Mark Twain

> "When I was a boy there was but one permanent ambition among my comrades [friends] in our village on the . . . Mississippi River. That was to be a Steamboatman."
> —Mark Twain

Steamboat races were popular events on the Mississippi River. These steamboats are docked in Cairo.

You dash onto the boat. *Brawny* crew members are wheeling crates from place to place. Passengers who traveled for the lowest-priced tickets are picking up their belongings. They sat between the bales and boxes during their journey. Above you, on their own special deck, other passengers are strolling toward the stairway. Crew members carry their bags.

ILLINOIS PORTRAIT

John Deere
1804–1886

John Deere's first factory.

John Deere was born in Rutland, Vermont. He traveled by canal boat, lake boat, and stagecoach to Illinois. There he designed a steel plow. To make the curved blade he cut a piece of an old saw blade and bent it around a log. It was sharp so it did not get clogged with dirt. Deere's self-scouring (self-cleaning) plow was a great success.

Later, one of Deere's partners said he was making too many changes in the design. Deere replied, "If we don't improve our product, someone else will."

Climbing to the upper deck you can't believe your eyes. The cabins are *luxurious*. Only the rich can afford to travel this way. Next to the cabins is the dining room. It has expensive wood on the walls and shiny brass railings.

The pilot blows the whistle once again. It's time for visitors to leave. From the dock, you watch the boat slip back onto the river. The calliope is playing again. Smoke billows from the stacks. The crew is busy making everything "ship shape" for the trip to the next stop. You wonder, could there be a more wonderful job in all the world than being a riverboat pilot?

Inventions Make Farming Easier

When farmers first came to the Illinois prairie they were not sure they had made the right choice. The soil was rich and fertile, but the grass was so thick it was hard to farm the land.

Cyrus McCormick's Reaper

Cyrus Hall McCormick moved to Chicago from Virginia. He wanted to help farmers cut the prairie grass and harvest their crops faster. All they had at the time was a tool called a scythe (SIth). It was a long curved blade with a handle.

McCormick invented a reaper that could be pulled by horses. It gathered the grain as it chopped. It let farmers harvest their crops five times faster than they could with the scythe. McCormick's reaper and the level Illinois prairie were made for each other. Soon he started a factory in Chicago to make the reapers.

Cyrus McCormick's reaper made harvesting much easier.

John Deere's Plow

Wooden plows could not cut through the thick roots of the tall grass. Iron plows were not much better. The rich prairie soil stuck to them like glue. A farmer had to stop plowing often to scrape soil from the plow.

John Deere was a blacksmith in Vermont who made farm tools. When he moved to Grand Detour, Illinois, he saw the farmers' problem. He wondered if he could make a plow that would clean itself. He made a curved steel blade from a broken saw. Farmers came to watch Deere try out his new self-*scouring* plow. It was a success! The soil slid right off the polished steel blade.

Later, Deere opened a factory in Moline. His business grew quickly. He advertised his invention all over the United States. Soon Deere's factory was making 10,000 plows per year.

With Deere's plow, Illinois farmers could plow large fields and plant large crops. With McCormick's reaper, they could harvest as much grain as they could plant. Wheat joined corn as a major crop. By 1850, Illinois produced more wheat than any other northern state.

John Deere invented the self-scouring plow.

Some farmers were worried that the steel might harm the soil.

Immigrants

Illinois was the fastest growing state in the country in 1850.

After the Black Hawk War, more land was available to settlers. The fear of Indian attacks was gone. Illinois was becoming a popular place. People who had moved here wrote letters to their relatives at home. They told of all the opportunities in Illinois.

In some European countries disease had ruined crops and the people were starving. Wars had destroyed their homes. Farmers there heard that land was inexpensive and fertile in Illinois. With hard work, they could make a good life.

Railroad companies had posted signs in countries such as England, Ireland, and Sweden. They wanted *immigrants* to come and work for them. They advertised cheap land and lots of jobs. They told people the land would be more expensive in the future, so they should buy right away. They promised the soil would never wear out.

Thousands of people left their homes and families to start a new life in America. Steamboats, canal boats, lake schooners, and stagecoaches took people to towns throughout Illinois.

Immigrants came for other reasons as well. Some came because they wanted to be able to practice their religion freely. The people heard that Americans could belong to any church they chose.

The Village of Bourbonnais

Religious groups came to Illinois and set up communities. First was the village of Bourbonnais. Bourbonnais was started near where Kankakee is today. It became the home of a group of Catholic French-Canadians who were unhappy with their lives in Canada.

The Mormons at Nauvoo

A group called the Mormons also came to Illinois to find religious freedom. Joseph Smith had organized this church in New York. They moved to Illinois after being driven out of Ohio and Missouri. They drained the swampland beside the Mississippi River and built the town of Nauvoo.

Thousands of Mormons came to Nauvoo. It soon became the largest town in Illinois. But neighbors did not like the way Mormons tried to **convert** them. Many feared that the Mormons were getting too powerful. They might soon control the state by voting as a group in elections. Others were troubled by the small army Smith had started in order to protect Nauvoo.

Because of all the trouble, Joseph Smith and his brother Hyrum were arrested. They were put in jail in Carthage. One evening a mob of people broke into the jail and killed them.

Mormon leader Joseph Smith was shot in Carthage.

This is historic Galena today. In pioneer times people rushed to Galena to work in the lead mines. They came from other states and from countries around the world. Galena became a busy mining town and shipping port. At one point Galena was the richest town in Illinois.

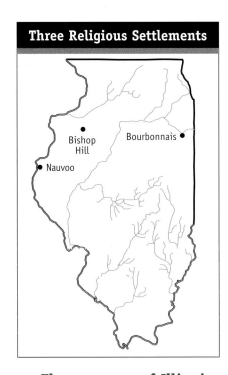

Three Religious Settlements

The governor of Illinois wrote a letter to the new Mormon leader, Brigham Young. He wrote, "If you can get off by yourself, you might enjoy peace not surrounded by such neighbors. I confess that I do not foresee the time when you will be permitted [allowed] to enjoy quiet."

In the winter of 1846 Brigham Young led the Mormons out of Nauvoo. They pulled their wagons across the frozen Mississippi River. After spending the winter in Iowa and Nebraska, they made the long journey to Utah, where they built Salt Lake City.

Bishop Hill

Bishop Hill was to be a perfect home for followers of Eric Jansson. The Janssonists were from Sweden. They did not agree with the state church of Sweden. But it was the only church allowed in Sweden at the time. After Jansson was put in jail (then later released), they decided they must leave Sweden.

Jansson led 300 followers to America, where they could live and worship in their own way. The journey was long and hard. They had to walk over 100 miles from Chicago into the Illinois prairie. They set up a village at Bishop Hill. First they built a church, which had apartments in it for some of the families. As more followers came to join them they added homes, parks, and stores to the village.

The people made linen, furniture, brooms, and wagons to sell. The Janssonist believed that a simple life was best.

A blacksmith at work in Bishop Hill.

Transportation Gets Even Better

Illinois leaders wanted to make travel around the state easier. They hired people to build roads and improve harbors and rivers. They started a canal and a railroad.

Illinois made big plans. But too many projects were started at one time. Illinois almost went broke. Imagine the following *debate* taking place in the Illinois *legislature*:

Mr. Somerville: Think of the good a railroad could bring to our farmers and craftsmen. No longer would they have to sell to their neighbors for whatever they could get. They could sell to people far from home.

A railroad would bring more factories to our state. Businesses would use it to sell goods to people all over the country. And more factories would mean more taxes and more jobs. Can we refuse our state this income? It needs it. I say we cannot.

A railroad would not freeze and become useless each winter, like a canal. Its path would not be limited. A railroad can be built to take the shortest routes. And speed! Imagine, goods and people moving along at a rate of fifteen miles an hour!

Mr. Swain: Do not be taken in by the fancy ideas of our friend Mr. Somerville. Our state does not have millions of dollars to spend on the wild ideas of *speculators*. Let them raise their own money to test their dreams.

What would happen once the road was built? Who could afford to buy the iron horses needed to use it? Certainly not the farmer or craftsman! You, my friends, would pay for it. And a few rich merchants would use it.

What we need, my friends, is a canal. Canals have already been proven. The Erie Canal has brought much trade to New York. The state is being well paid for the money it spent. Let our state put its money on a sure thing—a canal.

And that is what Illinois did.

The Illinois & Michigan Canal

In the past when people wanted to travel between Lake Michigan and the Illinois River they had to cross a narrow strip of land. Plans were made to build a canal through the strip of land. The canal would connect Lake Michigan to the Illinois River. Then there would be an all-water route from Lake Michigan to the Gulf of Mexico. The route would make shipping goods and traveling faster and cheaper.

Lake Michigan to the Gulf of Mexico

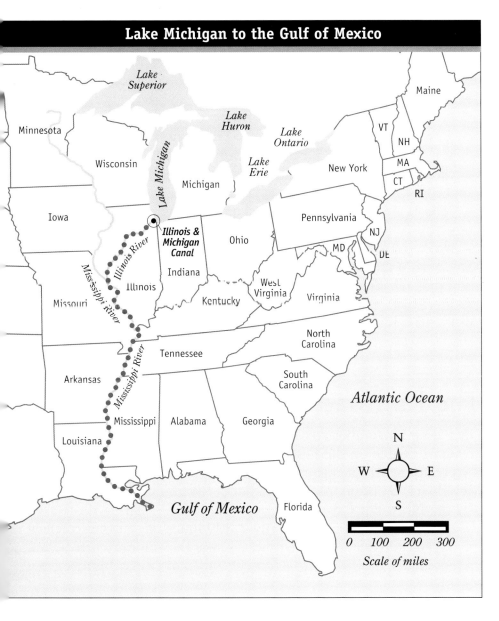

How Does a Canal Lock Work?

To make the trip between Chicago and the Illinois River, a boat had to pass through fifteen *locks*.

Locks raise or lower boats along their journey. Locks were needed because the water level of Lake Michigan is higher than the Illinois River at La Salle.

A lock is a space big enough to hold a canal boat, with huge doors on each end. When a boat needs to be raised, a door opens and the boat enters the lock. Then the door closes behind it. Water is let into the lock through the door in front of the boat. The water rises and lifts the boat. Water keeps running into the lock until the levels inside and outside are the same. The boat can now float out of the lock and continue its trip.

Can you see the doors on this early canal lock?

Building the Canal

Thousands of workers came to Illinois to build the canal. Many came from as far away as Ireland. They lived in *crude* camps. Diseases such as cholera and malaria often appeared because of unclean conditions and unsafe drinking water. For their labor, workers received about $1 per day. A workday lasted fourteen to fifteen hours.

Digging started in the town of Bridgeport, now part of Chicago. After twelve years workers reached the Illinois River at La Salle-Peru.

A Faster, Smoother Trip

Passengers once rode in stagecoaches at three or four miles per hour. Now they could zip along the canal at almost six miles per hour.

Speed was important to travelers, but so was comfort. The smooth canal was a nice change from rough roads. Canal boats were pulled steadily along by mules or horses walking on either side of the water. Travelers could sit on the top of the boats in good weather. They didn't have to sit inside a small coach with other passengers who smoked or snored loudly during the trip.

Passengers were the main cargo on the Illinois & Michigan Canal when it first opened. Later, when railroads came along, travelers switched again. The railroads were even faster. They could go where canals could not.

The boats were used to haul machinery, crops, and timber. Logs from Wisconsin were cut into boards in Chicago and shipped to farms and towns in many states. Wheat, corn, and beans were hauled from farms to Chicago, St. Louis, and New Orleans. Coal and other resources were put on boats headed for factories. Major products from towns along the canal's route, such as flour, wire, sand, and cement, were moved on canal boats.

The Railroad Boom

On a crisp November day in 1838 a steam *locomotive* took a tiny group of people on the first train ride in Illinois history. It carried the group eight miles to the end of its track. Then it returned to Meredosia, on the bank of the Illinois River. The railroad's name was the Northern Cross.

At that time there were only 2,800 miles of railroad track in the whole United States. Twenty years later the amount of track had increased to 30,000 miles. After the railroad came, Illinois grew quickly.

The Northern Cross Railroad

The Northern Cross Railroad was owned by the State of Illinois. Then Nicholas Ridgely bought it. Its track stretched from Meredosia to Springfield. Ridgely wanted the track to go to the Indiana border. But he had other things to think about at the same time. Because his two steam engines had been built in Pennsylvania, it took months for parts to get to Illinois. For almost a year, Ridgely's train cars had to be pulled by oxen and horses. His engines had broken down.

While Ridgely was finishing the tracks, another railroad company was just getting started. It planned to connect Galena with Chicago. It would also connect both towns with the southern end of the state. It would be called the Illinois Central Railroad.

The Illinois Central Railroad

The new company needed help to build its railroad. The company asked Illinois for money. The state gave the company land on both sides of the route. The Illinois Central Railroad could sell the land and use the money to pay for the building costs.

The company agreed to finish the railroad in six years. Company officials were sent to cities in the eastern United States and Europe to find workers. They hung posters in railroad stations, hotels, and places where new immigrants might see them. They would pay $1.25 a day in wages. Workers saw the signs and came to Illinois to lay the tracks.

Six years later, as promised, the last rail was put in place at Centralia. The longest railroad in the world was ready for travel.

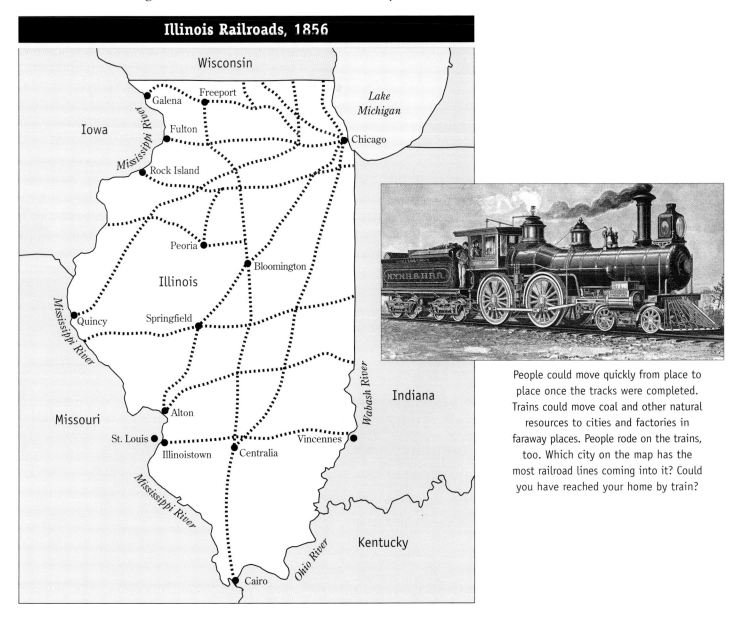

Illinois Railroads, 1856

People could move quickly from place to place once the tracks were completed. Trains could move coal and other natural resources to cities and factories in faraway places. People rode on the trains, too. Which city on the map has the most railroad lines coming into it? Could you have reached your home by train?

The Amish

Not everyone was excited about the new modern ways of transportation. A group of people called the Amish thought that all the *progress* that was going on didn't really make life better. They thought a simple life was best.

Around 1865, Amish families began moving into central Illinois. The Amish are a religious group that was founded by a man named Jakob Ammon in Switzerland. They thought the Mennonite Church they belonged to was becoming too concerned with worldly things. They wanted to live a simple life. They believed in values such as honesty, courtesy, and peace. They formed a group and moved to Pennsylvania in the 1600s.

Over time, some Amish families moved west to Ohio and then to Illinois. They settled in Arthur and Arcola. They made their living by farming the rich land. They planted wheat, oats, clover, and corn.

Today, several thousand Amish people live in Arthur, Arcola, Atwood, and Sullivan. They choose to keep the old way of life, riding in horse-drawn buggies and using gas lamps instead of electricity. If you visit these towns you will see quiet country roads, Amish homes and barns, small cottage businesses, and one-room schoolhouses.

Until just a few years ago the Amish made their living by farming. Now they also make and sell crafts, furniture, buggies, and quilts. They grow plants and herbs to sell. The people value honesty so much that in some stores the customer makes his or her own change from an open cash box.

The Amish people live a quiet simple life without cars, electricity, or fancy clothes.

activity

Come to Illinois!

Railroad companies tried to get workers by putting up posters that advertised Illinois. The posters told of cheap land, good soil, and growing towns.

Design your own poster advertising Illinois to people around the world. Include pictures and descriptions of all the things that make Illinois great.

Questions for Review

1. How did steamboats make travel better?

2. What farming tool did Cyrus McCormick invent?

3. What did John Deere invent?

4. List three reasons why immigrants left their homelands and came to Illinois.

5. Which religious group started the town of Nauvoo?

6. Which religious group started Bishop Hill?

7. What two bodies of water did the Illinois & Michigan Canal connect?

8. How did the new canal change travel?

9. List two towns where Amish people live today.

Geography Tie-In

Look at the map of the railroads on page 105. How do you think the railroad changed the animal and plant life in Illinois? How did it change life for people?

As a class, talk about the geography theme called "movement." Think of some ways the movement of goods and people changed because of the railroad.

THE TIME
1830–1870

PEOPLE TO KNOW
John Crenshaw
Owen Lovejoy
Elijah Lovejoy
U.S. President Abraham
    Lincoln
Mary Todd Lincoln
Stephen Douglas
Jennie Hodgers
Mary Ann Bickerdyke
U.S. President Ulysses
    Grant
Governor Richard Yates
John Wilkes Booth

PLACES TO LOCATE
Africa
Canada
Princeton
the South
the North
Kentucky
Indiana
Decatur
New Orleans
New Salem
Springfield
Gettysburg, Pennsylvania
Washington, D.C.
South Carolina
Galesburg
Cairo
Galena

timeline of events

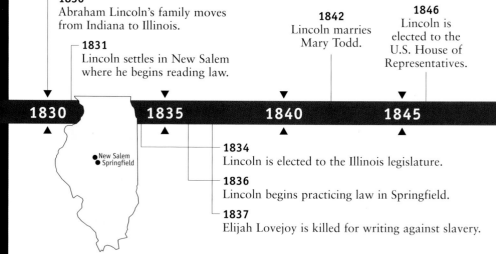

1830
Abraham Lincoln's family moves from Indiana to Illinois.

1831
Lincoln settles in New Salem where he begins reading law.

1842
Lincoln marries Mary Todd.

1846
Lincoln is elected to the U.S. House of Representatives.

1830 • New Salem • Springfield

1835   1840   1845

1834
Lincoln is elected to the Illinois legislature.

1836
Lincoln begins practicing law in Springfield.

1837
Elijah Lovejoy is killed for writing against slavery.

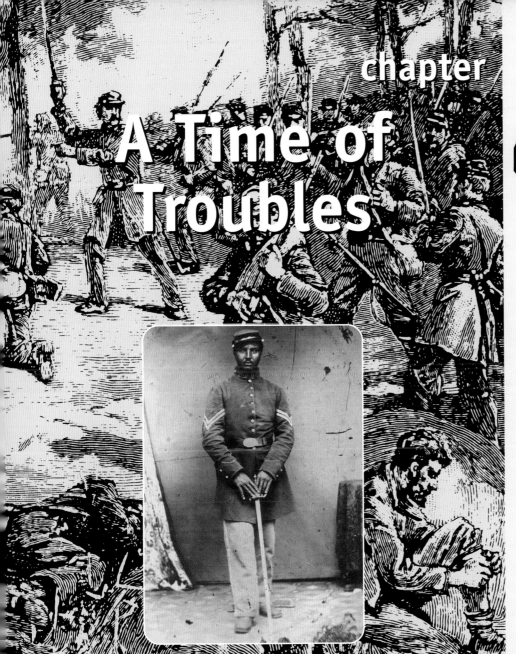

chapter 8

A Time of Troubles

TERMS TO UNDERSTAND

conflict
plantation
overseer
preserve
abolish
abolitionist
economy
Emancipation Proclamation
Gettysburg Address
secede
discourage
pension
enlist
shell
draft
debris

1860
Abraham Lincoln leaves Springfield to become president of the United States.

1861
Lincoln takes office on March 4th.
A group of southern states leaves the Union.

1863
January Lincoln issues the Emancipation Proclamation.
November Lincoln delivers the Gettysburg Address.

1864
Lincoln is re-elected as president.

1865
April 14 Lincoln is shot. He dies the next day

1850	1855	1860	1865	1870

1858
Lincoln-Douglas Debates

1861–1865
The Civil War

1850-1865
Some slaves escape to freedom on the Underground Railroad.

Slavery

As our state grew, so did the *conflict* over slavery. Illinois was a free state, but it was divided on the issue of slavery. Some people wanted to be able to keep slaves. Others thought all people should be free. If we take a look at slavery we can understand why this issue was tearing our state and country apart.

Imagine you are taking a walk, minding your own business. Suddenly, strange men surround you. You find yourself trapped. You're put in chains and forced to leave your home, your family, and everything that is familiar to you.

You march many miles with others who, like you, have been kidnapped and chained. Next you are forced down into the bottom of a ship. You live in horrible conditions as you travel for weeks across the ocean. There is not enough food or clean water. There is no fresh air. People are so crowded they can hardly move. You don't know where you are going or what the future holds.

That is how most slaves came to America. They were kidnapped from Africa and brought to America against their will. Slave traders sold them to *plantation* owners or anyone else who could pay the price. They would do hard work on the plantation without pay. They went from being free men and women to being someone's property. All of their children were also slaves.

"My brothers and sisters were bid off first . . . while my mother . . . held me by the hand. Then I was offered. My mother pushed through the crowd to the spot where [her master] was standing. She fell at his feet and clung to his knees, [begging] him in tones that only a mother can command, to buy her baby as well as herself and spare to her one, at least, of her little ones."
—Josiah Henson, runaway slave

Families were often split apart and sold to different owners at a slave auction. The slaves were sold to the highest bidder.

The Hard Life of a Slave

Most slaves lived on large sugar or cotton plantations in the South. From sunrise to sunset they worked for the plantation owner. When there was cotton to be picked, the *overseer* forced the people to work in the fields as soon as the sun came up.

Picking cotton was back-breaking work. For hours the slaves bent over the cotton plants in the hot sun. When it was time for a lunch of cold bacon or bread work stopped, but only for five or ten minutes. Then it was time to pick more cotton. Often the overseer used his whip to speed up the slower workers.

When it finally got too dark to see in the fields, it was time to weigh the cotton and do other chores. Wood needed to be cut. Tools needed to be fixed. Animals had to be cared for.

By late evening the slaves could prepare their suppers. They heated pork over a fire and baked cornmeal to eat with it. Supper ended the hard day. As they went to sleep, they dreamed of Sunday, the one day a week they could rest.

> *We [lived] in log huts, and on the bare ground. In a single room we were huddled, like cattle, ten or a dozen persons, men, women, and children. . . . Our beds were collections of old straw and old rags, thrown down in the corners and boxed in with boards; . . . The wind whistled and the rain and snow blew in through the cracks. . . the damp earth soaked in moisture till the floor was [muddy] as a pig sty.*
> —Josiah Henson

Some masters treated their slaves well. Others didn't think of them as people. They were very cruel. The people lived through each day with fear. If a slave had not picked enough cotton, he or she might be whipped. If a slave picked more than expected, there was another problem. The master might expect that much again the next day. Slaves could be sold at any time. They feared being sold to a master who was more cruel.

The Underground Railroad

The Underground Railroad was not really a railroad. It was a system of secret routes that slaves used to escape to free states in the North. It wasn't really underground, either. "Underground" just means that it was hidden from most people. The Underground Railroad had "stations," which were homes of people who hid the runaways. It also had "conductors," or people who helped the slaves get from station to station safely. There were Underground Railroad stations throughout the North all the way to Canada.

Learning to Read

Slaves were not allowed to learn to read. The owners were afraid that if their slaves learned to read and write they might write to slaves from other areas and unite against the masters. If the slaves could read maps and signs they might try to escape. Still, many slaves learned to read in secret. Being able to read was a way of saying to the masters, "You can never own my mind."

Some "conductors" had the slaves run away on a Saturday night so they wouldn't be missed until Sunday. The slave's owner couldn't put an ad in the paper until Monday. This gave runaways a two-day head start.

The Old Slave House

On top of Hickory Hill in southern Illinois sits the Crenshaw house. It was built in the 1830s by John Hart Crenshaw. For many years the house held a terrible secret.

While people around Illinois were risking their lives helping slaves escape, John Hart Crenshaw was kidnapping free black people and selling them into slavery. It was like the Underground Railroad in reverse.

The Crenshaw house became known as the Old Slave House. Many tourists have visited the Old Slave House to see the rooms where the kidnapped victims were hidden and sold.

Illinois Stations

Many stations on the Underground Railroad were right here in Illinois. One was in Princeton. It was the home of a preacher named Owen Lovejoy. He thought slavery was wrong. He had a large house with many closets. In the days of the Underground Railroad, the closets hid many escaped slaves. When night came the slaves hid under a pile of hay on a wagon. Then Lovejoy drove the wagon to the next station.

There are thirty-eight known stations in Illinois. They were in Quincy, Alton, Chester, Rockford, Chicago, and other towns. Today, people are working to have the sites *preserved*. They want to honor all the brave people who escaped and helped others escape.

> *The story of the Underground Railroad is a wonderful chapter in our history. Slaves took their lives in their hands, but whites who owned sites along the [secret] network. . . were very brave, too. The whole experience is something Americans can celebrate.*
> —Illinois Senator Carol Moseley-Braun

What do you think?

Why is it important to remember the terrible sad parts of history as well as the good parts? Do you think the Old Slave House is as important a landmark as the sites on the Underground Railroad? Why or why not?

RAN AWAY!

FROM THE SUBSCRIBER. **My Mulatto Boy, GEORGE.** Said George is 5 feet 8 inches in height, brown curly Hair, dark coat. I will give $400 for him alive, and the same sum for satisfactory proof that he has been killed.
Vide **ANTHONY & ELLIS' MAMMOTH** "UNCLE TOM'S CABIN." **WM. HARRIS.**

Posters like this one offered rewards for runaway slaves.

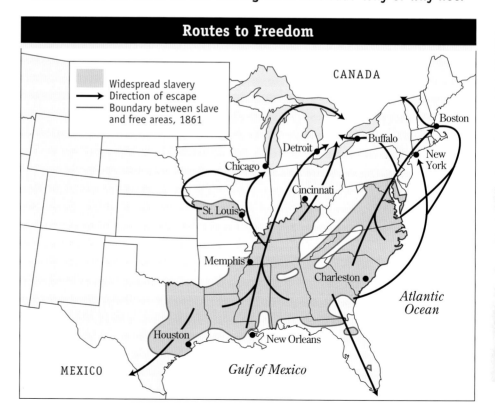

Routes to Freedom

Widespread slavery
→ Direction of escape
— Boundary between slave and free areas, 1861

CANADA

Boston

Buffalo

Detroit

New York

Chicago

Cincinnati

St. Louis

Memphis

Charleston

Atlantic Ocean

Houston

New Orleans

MEXICO

Gulf of Mexico

A State Divided

Many settlers had come to Illinois from southern states. They were used to slavery and saw nothing wrong with it. Others were not against slavery in the South, but they didn't want it in Illinois. Then there were people who wanted to end or *abolish* slavery everywhere. These people were called *abolitionists*. No matter what side they were on, people had very strong feelings about slavery.

Elijah Lovejoy

Owen Lovejoy's brother Elijah was a newspaper editor. He also believed strongly that slavery was wrong. He spoke out against it in his paper. His views made some people angry — so angry that they became violent. Twice a mob attacked him for writing against slavery. They broke into his office and ruined his printing press.

Lovejoy moved from St. Louis, Missouri, to Alton, Illinois, to escape the mobs. But he was no safer in Illinois. Again mobs destroyed his new printing press. They threw it into the river. They told him there would be more violence if he kept attacking slavery in his newspaper. Lovejoy was not willing to give up. He ordered yet another printing press. As soon as it arrived, the mob attacked again. This time they killed Lovejoy.

Alton

A mob attacked Elijah Lovejoy's office. They were angry at him for writing against slavery.

Stuck in the Middle

New York City
•

• Richmond

Here's a quick quiz: Is Illinois a southern state or a northern state?

Congratulations—you're right! It's both. Its southern tip is farther south than Richmond, Virginia. Virginia is a southern state. Illinois' northern border is as far north as New York City. New York is a northern state. Illinois sided with the North in the Civil War.

A Nation Divided

The conflicts that were dividing Illinois were dividing the entire country. All of these conflicts were about freedom and rights.

States' Rights

One conflict was over what rights a state should have. People in the South thought the states should have more power than the national government. They were worried about the government having too much control over them.

People in the North thought the national government should have certain powers over the states. They thought that some really important rules should be the same all across the nation.

Slavery

As you know, another important conflict was slavery. Many people, mostly in the South, owned slaves. Many people in the North felt it was wrong for anyone to own another person. Others felt it was up to each state to decide if they wanted to allow slavery.

There were also new territories trying to become states. Southerners wanted the new states to allow slavery. Northerners wanted the new states to be free.

Economics

Many Southerners said slavery was important to their *economy*. The people were mainly farmers. The crops they grew, such as cotton, tobacco, rice, and sugar, needed many fieldworkers. The farmers thought their way of life depended on slavery.

The people who owned slaves were rich plantation owners. Their slaves were a measure of their success. If the slaves worked hard, there was plenty of cotton to sell. This cotton was sold to clothing manufacturers in many countries. Then plantation owners could use the money to buy more land.

In the North, people worked in other industries. Thousands of people in northern cities worked in factories. They also worked to build canals and railroads. Some people worked for themselves making barrels, wagons, and other goods for the factory, home, or farm. There were many farms, but they were smaller. In most cases the families could do the work themselves. When the steel plow and the reaper became widely used, farmers could plant and harvest more without adding more workers.

For years the people of the North and South lived with their differences. But as more territories were trying to become states, these questions did not go away. Would the new states allow slavery?

Abraham Lincoln

Abraham Lincoln was born in Kentucky in a log cabin on a small farm. He lived there for the first seven years of his life. Then the Lincolns moved to Indiana. They left Kentucky for two reasons. First, Abraham's father Thomas lost his farm. The second reason was slavery. Kentucky was a slave state. Thomas Lincoln believed it was wrong to own slaves.

The land the Lincolns settled on in Indiana was in the forest. Abraham helped his father clear the forest and build a new log cabin. There was so much work to do that there was little time for education. When there was time, there was not always a school open. Books and paper were hard to find, too. Lincoln did his lessons on a smooth wooden board. He wrote with a piece of charcoal. He went to several different schools for short periods of time. In all, he spent no more than one year in school. Still, he learned to read, write, and work with numbers. He borrowed books from anyone he could and read them by the fireside.

Lincoln became well known in his town. He grew to be a very tall young man and a good strong worker. This made him a favorite among other farm families. Whenever he could be spared from his father's farm, he did work for his neighbors. People noticed that he was a good speaker. Everyone liked to hear him tell stories.

"A friend is someone who finds me a new book to read."
—Abraham Lincoln

Lincoln was born in Kentucky in this log cabin.

Lincoln Comes to Illinois

When Lincoln was about twenty-one years old his family moved to Illinois. They bought a farm near Decatur. Again, Abraham helped his family get started on the new farm. A year later, Lincoln began life on his own. He was hired to help take a flatboat down the Mississippi River to New Orleans. While in New Orleans he saw a slave auction. He thought it was horrible.

Back in Illinois, the flatboat owner was pleased with Lincoln's work. He hired Lincoln to work in a store in New Salem. When he was not busy, Lincoln spent time reading and studying. He borrowed books, read newspapers, and talked with people to learn as much as he could. Honest, brave, and friendly, Lincoln quickly made many friends.

Lincoln worked at several different jobs over the next few years. With a friend, he bought and ran a store. They sold tea, coffee, sugar, salt, hats, and shoes to the people of New Salem. But in a few months the store failed. It took several years for Lincoln to pay off the debts from the store. Then he took a job as postmaster (the person in charge of the post office) for New Salem. He also began to study law while in New Salem.

"Honest Abe"

The people of New Salem liked Lincoln and knew they could trust him. One story says that a woman once overpaid him by six cents. When Lincoln realized that he had been overpaid he walked six miles to return the money. You can see how he earned the nickname "Honest Abe."

Lincoln was famous for his sense of humor as well as his honesty. One time two men came to Lincoln to have an argument settled. They could not agree on how long a person's legs should be. One thought longer legs were better. The other argued for shorter legs. When they asked Lincoln for his opinion, he said: "After much thought, considering all the issues, I believe a person's legs ought to be long enough to reach from his body to the ground."

Lincoln was shy around women, but when he was thirty years old he met Mary Todd. They got married and had four sons. Mary once said of her husband, ". . . his heart is as large as his arms are long." They were very proud of their sons. When one of them was sick, Lincoln sat up with him night after night. Sadly, three of the boys died at a young age. Only the oldest, Robert Todd Lincoln, lived past the age of twenty-one.

Abraham Lincoln went from being a poor farmer in the backwoods to the president of the United States. He taught himself almost everything he knew. His leadership kept the nation together through the Civil War. His *Emancipation Proclamation* freed the slaves. Lincoln's words inspired the whole country again in a speech called the *Gettysburg Address*. That speech, which he wrote while riding the train to Gettysburg, Pennsylvania, became his most famous. It reminded everyone how strongly he believed in the ideas our country was founded on.

Just five days after the Civil War ended, Lincoln went to see a play at Ford's Theater in Washington, D.C. During the play, Lincoln was shot. The next day he died. He will always be remembered as one of our greatest presidents.

". . . his heart is as large as his arms are long."
—Mary Todd Lincoln

This statue of a strong young Lincoln is in New Salem.

Statue photos by Karen I. Hirsch ▶

This is how New Salem looked
when Lincoln lived there.

President Abraham Lincoln is often called the
"Great Emancipator" because he freed the slaves.
This statue is in Springfield.

After Abraham Lincoln married
Mary Todd they moved to this
home in Springfield.

New Salem is
a small town near
Springfield.

It has been said that Lincoln was too poor to pay for a ride to the state capital. According to the story, he once walked almost 100 miles from his home in New Salem to the state capitol in Vandalia.

Lincoln tried cases at the Mt. Pulaski Courthouse.

Lincoln Enters Politics

The first time Abe Lincoln ran for political office he lost. But he tried again. This time he was elected to serve in the Illinois legislature, where the laws are made. While serving in the legislature, Lincoln studied hard and became a lawyer. Three times he was elected to the legislature. There he made his first speeches against slavery.

Lincoln worked at this law office. Notice the stove for heat and the candles for light.

Lincoln-Douglas Debates

In 1858 two Illinois men debated the questions of the day. One was Stephen A. Douglas, a senator running for re-election. He was a short man whom people called the "Little Giant." People all over the country knew of him.

Hoping to take Douglas's job as senator was Abraham Lincoln, a lawyer at the time. Few people outside the state knew Lincoln.

The debates were popular events. Brass bands played and cannons boomed. Thousands of people came from nearby towns and farms.

The two men represented the ideas of people all over Illinois and the country. Lincoln believed that slavery was evil. It should not be allowed to spread. "The real issue," he said, was the "struggle between right and wrong." Douglas said that Lincoln was trying to start a war. "Let the people speak!" Douglas said. He believed the white people in each territory should decide if they wanted to own slaves.

The two great men debated the slavery question in Alton, Charleston, Freeport, Galesburg, Jonesboro, Ottawa, and Quincy. On election day, Senator Douglas was re-elected.

This monument in Quincy shows the Lincoln-Douglas Debate that took place there.

Photo by John Lynn

The President from Illinois

The battle wasn't over. Now Lincoln was known all over the country. Two years later, he and Douglas met again. This time each wanted to be president of the United States. This time, Lincoln won. In November of 1860 he was elected to be our sixteenth president. Lincoln took his wife, Mary, and their sons to Washington, D.C. to live in the White House.

Abraham Lincoln was the first U.S. president to be elected from Illinois.

The Civil War

People in the South did not like Lincoln's ideas. They did not want him to lead the country. They had said that if he became president, their states would leave the Union and form their own nation.

Not long after Lincoln won, South Carolina left the Union. Other states followed. Abraham Lincoln had not yet taken office and already seven states had *seceded* from the Union. They called themselves the Confederate States of America, or the Confederacy.

"A house divided against itself cannot stand."
—Abraham Lincoln

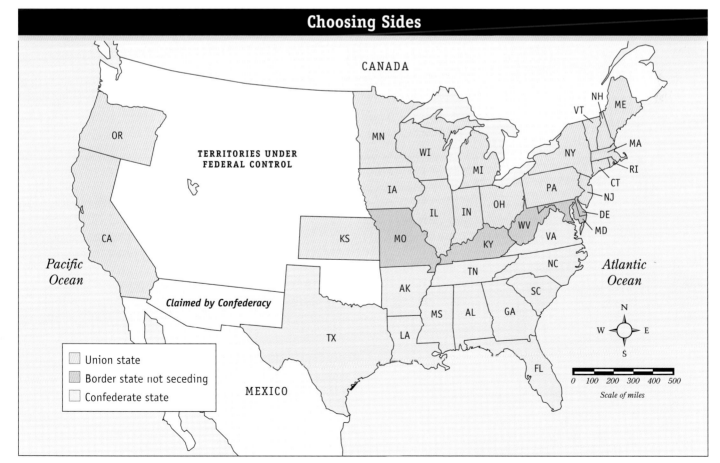

Choosing Sides

CANADA

TERRITORIES UNDER FEDERAL CONTROL

Claimed by Confederacy

MEXICO

Pacific Ocean

Atlantic Ocean

OR, CA, MN, WI, MI, IA, IL, IN, OH, NY, PA, VT, NH, ME, MA, RI, CT, NJ, DE, MD, WV, VA, KS, MO, KY, TN, NC, SC, AK, MS, AL, GA, TX, LA, FL

N W E S

0 100 200 300 400 500
Scale of miles

Union state
Border state not seceding
Confederate state

A civil war is a war where people from the same nation fight each other.
The northern states were called the Union. The southern states were called the Confederacy.

War Songs

During the Civil War a Chicago man named George F. Root wrote several war songs. Union soldiers sang his songs around campfires and on the battlefields. Songs such as *A Battle Cry of Freedom* helped keep spirits up. War songs helped in another way. Hearing soldiers singing together often **discouraged** those on the other side.

Many black men volunteered to fight in the Union army.

This is Jennie Hodgers as Albert Cashier.

People all over the country waited to see what President Lincoln would do. In his first speech he said he did not plan to change the South. He would not try to end slavery there. He also said that he did not plan to fight. But he said he would not give up any of the forts he held in the South.

Fort Sumter in South Carolina was one of the forts Lincoln refused to give up. Confederate soldiers fired on the fort. No one on either side was killed, but the South won the first battle in the Civil War.

It was time for the southern states that had not seceded to choose sides. Four more states joined the Confederacy. Four slave states stayed in the Union.

A Call for Soldiers

Lincoln asked for volunteers to defend the Union. The rush of young men from Illinois was greater than anyone had expected. Sometimes whole groups of teachers, firemen, or lead miners signed up.

At first, blacks were not allowed in the army. But after two years they were allowed to join. About 1,800 blacks from Illinois went to war.

Women in the War

Women helped by setting up hospitals, making bandages and clothing for the troops, and raising money. Some women, who felt they were not doing enough, dressed themselves as men and became spies or soldiers.

Jennie Hodgers

Women were not allowed to be soldiers in the Civil War. But that didn't stop Jennie Hodgers. She joined the 95th Illinois Volunteers and fought for three years. How did she do it? She joined as "Albert Cashier," a man.

Jennie Hodgers fought in many battles while she was in the army. After the war she was qualified to receive a **pension**. A pension is money that is paid to a person every month. But she worried that she might not get the money if the army found out she was a woman. She remained Albert Cashier until she was killed in an accident many years later.

Historians believe that as many as 400 women may have served as men in the Union and Confederate armies.

"Mother" Bickerdyke

Mary Ann Bickerdyke became famous for her service in the war. She worked so hard she was called the "Mother" of the Union army.

Mrs. Bickerdyke had been a nurse. While in church one Sunday, she heard about the awful conditions in army hospitals. One week later, Bickerdyke was on a train headed to Cairo. She had medical supplies, which she had collected from members of her church.

Mrs. Bickerdyke arrived in Cairo and went to the army hospital. What she saw made her angry. The hospital was just three tents. In each tent were ten men and two or three cots. The others had to sleep on straw on the ground. The straw had not been changed in weeks. The men were covered with dirt and flies. Their clothes had not been washed since they had arrived. The only supplies in the tents were buckets of water.

Mrs. Bickerdyke thought about what to do. She walked over to a group of healthy soldiers and asked them to follow her. They said they couldn't go unless they were given an order by one of their officers. But this wasn't going to stop her. She offered them a bribe: if they helped her clean up the hospital, she would cook them a chicken dinner.

The soldiers rounded up some barrels and sawed them in half. They scrubbed them with lye soap. Then they filled them with hot water. They brought the patients out from the tents and removed their tattered clothes. Each patient had his face and head shaved. Then the men were given hot baths and washed down with lye soap. The tents were cleaned out and the men returned to clean quarters in clean clothes.

Bickerdyke followed the same routine at many hospitals. She even started a new army hospital in Cairo. Soon soldiers along the Mississippi and Ohio Rivers were all calling her "Mother."

Mother Bickerdyke could also get tough. At one hospital she made a new kitchen. She filled the shelves with food her friends back in Galesburg had prepared. In a few days she noticed items were missing. She suspected that some of the kitchen workers were helping themselves to the supplies. To catch the guilty workers, Mother baked a peach pie and left it on the window sill to cool. She told the workers it was for the patients, so it must not be touched.

The temptation was too great. When Mother returned she found the pie half eaten. Without a word, Mrs. Bickerdyke went to do chores in another room. Soon the kitchen workers began to show up at the hospital with stomach aches. Mother had put herbs in the pie that caused sore stomachs. It was easy to pick out the kitchen thieves.

ILLINOIS PORTRAIT

"Mother" Bickerdyke
1817–1901

Mary Ann Ball Bickerdyke was born in Ohio, but moved to Galesburg, Illinois. When the Civil War began she wanted to do her part. She moved to Cairo and worked as a volunteer nurse. For four years she tended soldiers in hospitals up and down the Mississippi River. She used her good sense and energy to improve their health and comfort. She baked them bread, cleaned their tents, and brought in new supplies. Mother Bickerdyke was one of many strong women who served in the Civil War. Today, there is a monument in her honor at Galesburg.

ILLINOIS PORTRAIT

Ulysses S. Grant
1822–1885

Ulysses Grant was born in Ohio. He moved to Galena, Illinois, about when the Civil War began. When there was a call for troops to fight in the Union army, Grant signed up to be an officer. He gathered volunteers from Galena and other towns. After showing great leadership, he was put in charge of the volunteer soldiers at Cairo. Grant gained more and more responsibilities in the army. He rose to be the general of the Union army. He helped win important victories for the North and end the Civil War. Later he served as president of the United States.

Young Boys Go to War

Most soldiers were at least eighteen years old, but some younger boys went to war as well. In the North, boys as young as nine years old were buglers in the army. Other boys who went to visit their fathers stayed on to fight. Many lied about their age so they could fight in the war. Later, the Confederacy passed a law allowing boys under eighteen to *enlist*. Some boys as young as eleven years old joined the battles.

Young boys soon learned that being in the army meant a lot more marching than fighting. They marched for miles and miles through mud and dust, in the rain, in the heat, and in the cold. They slept in tents or sometimes just out on the cold wet ground. Often they had to share blankets.

Many of the boys became homesick and scared. The battles were terrible and frightening. Many boys saw their friends wounded or killed. Elisha Stockwell described what he was feeling in the middle of a battle:

I want to say, as we lay there and the shells were flying over us, my thoughts went back to my home, and I thought what a foolish boy I was to run away and get into such a mess as I was in.

After the war, the government changed its rules. The Civil War was the last time large numbers of boys so young fought for our country.

This boy joined the army when he was ten years old. He was the youngest soldier in the Union army.

The War Drags On

Both sides thought the war would be short. In the South, soldiers were asked to serve for no more than a year. Lincoln asked for even less. He called for 75,000 soldiers to serve for three months.

But the war went on. As it got longer, fewer soldiers signed up. Both sides had to *draft* men in order to get enough soldiers. Governor Richard Yates of Illinois helped. Yates was a friend to the soldiers. He told them they would not be forgotten. He kept his word. Again and again, Yates visited hospitals and war camps to lift the soldiers' spirits.

A Day of Freedom Comes

President Lincoln tried to end the horrible war. He tried to solve the slavery problem. He offered to pay slave owners for any slaves they would free. Not one state took his offer. Lincoln had even asked the Confederate states to come back into the Union without freeing their slaves. They refused. Finally, in January, 1863, Lincoln issued the Emancipation Proclamation. In this official paper he freed the slaves in the Confederacy. It was a day of great rejoicing. Black people would be free to build their own lives. They sang "Thank God, I'm free at last!"

Peace and Freedom at Last

For four long years Americans fought one another. At first the South had won many battles. But the North was better able to fight a long war. Finally the South surrendered. The Civil War was over. Over a half million men and women had lost their lives. The North had won, and the states joined together again.

The Country Loses a Great Leader

Lincoln had been re-elected as president near the end of the war. He wanted the states to come back together quickly and peacefully, and he wanted to rebuild the South. He hoped to "bind up the nation's wounds" and bring about a "lasting peace."

But Abraham Lincoln never had a chance. Just five days after the war ended he was shot. John Wilkes Booth, an actor, shot Lincoln in a Washington, D.C. theater. The next morning the president was dead.

The entire country was very sad to lose such a great man. Lincoln's coffin was put on a special train that would bring him back to Illinois. Crowds of people stood beside the tracks to salute him as the train went by.

Illinois' Contribution to the Civil War

- 260,000 men and women from Illinois were soldiers or nurses.
- 30,000 Illinois men lost their lives fighting to save the Union.
- Grain and beef from Illinois fed the Union soldiers.
- Cairo was a major base for the Union army.
- Abraham Lincoln and Ulysses Grant were very important to the Civil War.

Tragedy on the *Sultana*

The worst steamboat disaster in history took place on a cold April night in 1865. The *Sultana* had just left Memphis, Tennessee, on the Mississippi River. Its cargo was Union soldiers.

The soldiers had just been released from prison camps in the South. Many were sick and weak. They were traveling north to Cairo. They were going home.

For two hours that night the overcrowded boat strained against the river's current. The river was full from heavy rains. Then, it happened. The boat's boilers exploded. The explosion could be heard back in Memphis. Soldiers and *debris* filled the river. When morning came, rescuers counted more than 1,500 soldiers dead from drowning or burns.

activity

Cause and Effect

Whenever we do something there is an effect, or result. For example, when we enter a dark room and flip on the light switch, the room is filled with light. This is called cause and effect. The cause is flipping on the light switch. The effect is that the room is filled with light. Life is filled with cause-and-effect relationships.

As we study Illinois history it is important to understand cause and effect. This will give us a better picture of our history.

CAUSE: Something that happened first, and caused something else to happen

EFFECT: What happened as a result of the cause

Look at each pair of sentences below. On a separate piece of paper, write 'C' for the cause and 'E' for the effect. Look back in the chapter if you need help.

EXAMPLE:

  _C_   Elijah Lovejoy printed articles saying that slavery was wrong.

  _E_   Many people were angry at Lovejoy's views.

1. ____ Farmers in the South planted huge crops of cotton.

    ____ They needed workers to pick the cotton.

2. ____ A slave girl is caught learning to read.

    ____ She is punished by the "master."

3. ____ Some slaves made it to freedom.

    ____ Brave people risked their lives to escape from slavery.

4. ____ Lincoln loved to read books and newspapers.

    ____ Lincoln could talk about many different subjects.

5. ____ Eleven southern states left the Union.

    ____ Lincoln was elected president.

6. ____ Confederate troops fired on Fort Sumter.

    ____ The North and South went to war for four years.

Questions for Review

1. Why did farmers in southern states want to own slaves?
2. Why did people think that slavery was wrong?
3. What was the Underground Railroad?
4. List the three main conflicts that were dividing the country.
5. What jobs did Abraham Lincoln have when he lived in New Salem?
6. Abraham Lincoln and Stephen Douglas met in several Illinois towns to debate what issue?
7. After Lincoln became president, seven states left the Union. What did they call themselves?
8. How did women help in the war?
9. How long did the Civil War last?
10. What happened to President Lincoln five days after the war ended?

Many Civil War soldiers are buried in this cemetery in Mound City.

Geography Tie-In

Look at the map on page 119. Use the map key to figure out what kinds of states surrounded Illinois. Were they Union states, border states, Confederate states? What kinds of problems might the "border states" have faced?

THE TIME
1779–2000

PEOPLE TO KNOW
Jean du Sable
Gurdon Hubbard
Upton Sinclair
Marshall Field
Montgomery Ward
Richard Sears
George Pullman
Patrick O'Leary
Potter Palmer
William Jenney
Louis Sullivan
Frank Lloyd Wright
George Ferris
Dwight Moody
Jane Addams

PLACES TO LOCATE
Chicago
Lake Michigan
Chicago River
Wisconsin
Minnesota
Cedarville
Des Plaines River

Chicago had very few buildings in 1820.
Compare the two photos to see how the city has changed.

1779
Du Sable sets up a trading post at the mouth of the Chicago River.

1865
Union Stock Yard is built. Marshall Field opens the first department store.

timeline of events

| 1780 | 1790 | 1800 | 1860 | 1870 | 1880 |

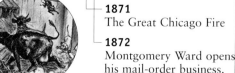

1871
The Great Chicago Fire

1872
Montgomery Ward opens his mail-order business.

The Growth of Chicago

9

(Photo by Karen Hirsch)

TERMS TO UNDERSTAND

destination
grain elevator
stockyard
refine
union
strike
pardon
architect
culture
exposition
charity
elevated
ethnic

1885 William Jenney builds the first skyscraper.

1886 Haymarket Square Riot

1889 Jane Addams opens Hull House.

1894 Pullman Strike

1973
The Sears Tower is built.

| 1890 | 1900 | 1910 | 1920 | 1930 | 1970 | 1980 | 1990 | 2000 |

1893
Chicago hosts the
World's Fair.

1900
A new canal reverses the
flow of the Chicago River.

1888–1910
Elevated streetcar tracks,
known as the El, are built.

South Water Street, Chicago, 1834. The picture shows a few homes and other buildings. What else can you see in the picture that gives clues about what life was like then?

From Village to City

From the beginning, Chicago was almost certain to become an important city. Its location had always been a busy one. For hundreds of years American Indians walked across this spot. They carried their canoes from Lake Michigan to inland rivers. Later Jean du Sable built his trading post in the same place. Traffic to and from the trading post was busy. Even after the Fort Dearborn Massacre, people returned to settle at the mouth of the Chicago River. From that point on the town grew.

Chicago was a good place to do business because it was near Lake Michigan. Materials from other states could easily be brought there by ship. Goods made in Chicago could be shipped out to many places.

As businesses grew, so did the need for workers. People came to Chicago to find work. Settlers were buying land like crazy. Men with land to sell waited for boats to dock, then rushed to the people and tried to get them to buy. As the number of people grew, so did the need for goods and services. In other words, growth led to more growth.

Trains brought wheat and corn from Illinois farms to Chicago's many grain elevators.

Early Chicago Industries

Farming had been the way most people in Illinois made their living. More and more, industry was catching up to farming. One thing that helped industry grow was the railroad.

The Railroad

After trains were invented, people and goods could travel much faster than they did on canal boats. All over the country, companies began laying track.

In Illinois, railroads connected northern cities like Galena, Freeport, and Rock Island to southern cities like Alton, Centralia, and Cairo. The tracks passed through Quincy, Peoria, Springfield, and Bloomington. Much of the time, Chicago was their *destination*. From all directions, waterways and railroads led to Chicago. Like beads on a string, towns developed along the railroads.

Chicago became the world's largest railroad center. Over 100 trains entered or left the city every day. They brought wheat and corn to the flour mills and *grain elevators* of Chicago. Soon it became the nation's most important grain market. Trains also brought people to Chicago. Most of the newcomers were immigrants from Europe and other countries.

Photo by John Lynn

The Meat-Packing Industry

Farmers moved their pigs and cattle by train to Chicago, where they were butchered and sold. The meat was shipped in refrigerated railroad cars to other towns and cities. Then a man named Gurdon Hubbard got the idea to build a huge warehouse in Chicago to store the meat from the animals. His idea was a success.

Packing and storing meat became big business. Soon there were *stockyards* around the city. To make things easier, the Union Stock Yard and Transit Company was started. The company built hundreds of pens for the animals. They bought railroads, a bank, and a hotel. Chicago's new stockyard brought a lot of business. It was the home of companies such as Swift, Armour, and Cudahy.

A writer named Upton Sinclair told the story of an immigrant who worked in the Chicago stockyards. His book described the unclean conditions that were common as the meat-packing industry grew. Because of his book the meat-packing industry was forced to make things cleaner and safer.

"There would be meat stored in great piles in rooms; and the water from the leaky roofs would drip over it, and thousands of rats would race about on it. . . . The packers would put poisoned bread out for them, they would die, and then the rats, bread, and meat would go into the hoppers together."
—from *The Jungle*

The Union Stock Yards helped make Chicago the meat-packing capital of the world.

Farm Machinery

Farming has always been hard work. People wanted more and more machines to help make the work easier and faster. John Deere had built a factory in Moline, where he could get the steel he needed to build his plows. Cyrus McCormick, who had invented the reaper, moved to Chicago. He built the largest factory in the city. Inventors began to make and sell other helpful farm tools, such as barbed wire for fences.

ILLINOIS PORTRAIT

Marshall Field
1834–1906

Marshall Field was born in Massachusetts. He moved to Chicago when he was twenty-two. He worked as a clerk in a dry goods store. Over the next nine years he worked his way up to become a partner in the business. Years later, he bought out his partners and started Marshall Field and Company. His department store was a great success. As Field's business grew, so did his wealth. Near the end of his life he gave one million dollars to start the Field Museum of Natural History. It is one of the best natural history museums in the world.

The slogan for Marshall Field's was "Give the lady what she wants!"

Iron, Steel, and Other Riches

Chicago's people wanted to keep the industry boom going. But they needed iron and steel to do this. Iron ore had just been discovered in Minnesota. Once again, Chicago's location on Lake Michigan helped business. It was easy for ships from Minnesota to carry the iron ore through the Great Lakes to Chicago.

Companies such as the Chicago Iron Company and the Joliet Iron and Steel Company started building furnaces to make iron and steel. Illinois became a leading producer of steel.

The railroads could bring coal, clay, limestone, sand, gravel, and fluorite from Illinois towns to Chicago. Lumber mills were built to turn logs brought from Wisconsin and Minnesota into lumber for building.

Steel is Strong

Iron was an important metal for making things that people used every day. Then people learned how to use iron to make steel. Steel was stronger than iron and it didn't rust easily.

To make steel, iron ore is burned in huge furnaces. Limestone, oxygen, coal, and scrap metal are mixed with the burning iron. As the mixture burns the bad parts are separated out. Then it is cooled down into finished or *refined* steel.

Steel was used in tall buildings, farm machinery, railroad cars, tracks, and engines. Today, steel is used to make cars, refrigerators, vacuum cleaners, wire, and much more.

Department Stores

Chicago is the home of the modern department store. It was started by Marshall Field and two other men. They owned a small store in Chicago. They stocked the best goods they could find. There were furs, carpets, and the latest fashions. They invited store owners in small towns to buy from the store. The owners could come to Chicago and pick out items they wanted for their own stores.

The other men left the business, but Field kept it going. His store was famous for service to its customers. Shoppers were greeted by a doorman. The clerks were trained to be friendly and helpful. Inside the store there was a library, a children's playroom, a restaurant, and a telegraph office.

Photo by John D. Ivanko

This is Marshall Field's today.

Goods that customers bought at the store could even be delivered to their homes.

Buying by Mail

Shopping by mail from catalogs brought department store goods to villages and farms. The best at this business were Montgomery Ward and Richard Sears.

Ward arrived in Chicago at the age of twenty-three. He worked for Marshall Field as a salesman traveling to hundreds of small towns. Ward wondered why the same railroads taking him from place to place couldn't haul goods sold through a catalog. He opened a mail-order business. It began with a one-page catalog of household goods. Soon he was the number-one supplier for farm families all over the country. Another mail-order company, Sears and Roebuck, moved to Chicago years later.

The goods in the catalogs were cheaper than in the department stores. The catalogs were filled with drawings and descriptions of the items. They explained clearly how people should measure themselves to order things that would fit. People could buy almost anything through the mail. Furs, eye glasses, medicine, wigs, cars, and even houses (lumber and plans) have been in the catalogs.

Boys' fashions are shown on this page from a 1927 Sears and Roebuck Catalogue.

Problems on the Job

Some people who had started the new industries became rich. They lived in huge houses and dressed in expensive clothes. But the people who worked in the factories received low wages and worked long hours.

There were few laws in those days that said how factory workers should be treated. Many factory owners did not care much about the workers. They did not try to give them a nice place to work. They pushed them to make more, faster. The people worked twelve to fourteen hours a day in factories that were often unsafe and unhealthy. They were paid very low wages. If anyone complained, he or she was fired. There were so many other people looking for jobs that the owners could easily find someone else.

Workers began to come together and fight for change. Coal miners, railroad workers, iron makers, tailors, and other workers formed *unions*. They tried to get the General Assembly to make laws about how long the workday could be. As a result, Illinois was the first state to make a law that said people only had to work eight hours a day.

One way workers tried to change poor working conditions was to go on *strike*. Often the strikes led to violence.

Coal miners went on strike in Virden. When the company simply replaced them with other workers, fighting broke out.

Riot at Haymarket Square

The workers at McCormick's reaper factory went on strike. Fighting broke out and the police shot several men. The labor leaders called for an open meeting, or rally, at Haymarket Square. When the police tried to break up the crowd, a bomb was thrown. It killed seven policemen.

No one knows who threw the bomb, but eight men were arrested. They were tried and found guilty. Some of the men were hung. Some went to prison. Years later, the governor *pardoned* the men still in prison. He said that no evidence had ever been shown to connect them to the bombing.

The Pullman Strike

George Pullman invented the railroad sleeping car. His sleeping cars were made in his Chicago factory. Pullman thought of a way to avoid strikes and unhappy workers. He would build a town for his workers where they could live a safe and comfortable life. He built apartments, stores, parks, churches, and factories in his town. He named it Pullman, after himself.

But the workers were not happy. Pullman owned everything in the town. He controlled the prices. He made the rent higher than it was in Chicago. When business slowed down, he cut the workers' wages but he would not lower their rent. The workers felt it was unfair. Their union went on strike. Fighting broke out. Pullman's dream town turned into a disaster.

What do you think?

• How long are you in school each day? Most businesses still have an eight-hour workday. Many people work overtime. Do you think eight hours is too long or too short for adults to be at work?

• Talk to adults you know about some problems at work today. How can we make places of work better?

The Great Chicago Fire

A "city of wood" is how Chicago could have been described in 1871. It had wooden houses and wooden barns with wooden roofs. Downtown buildings up to six stories tall were built out of wood. Sidewalks were made of wood. Even the streets were paved with wooden blocks.

Almost no rain had fallen on Chicago since the beginning of summer. Everything was dry. The stage was set for a terrible fire.

The O'Leary's Cow

Tragedy began in a barn behind Patrick O'Leary's cottage, just south of downtown. It was just after 9:00 P.M. The O'Learys had already gone to bed. Legend says that a cow kicked over a lantern and started the barn on fire.

Very soon the fire was out of control. Fanned by a strong wind, it spread quickly toward downtown. Chicago's firemen were already weary from fighting fires the night before. Some of their equipment was no longer working. The firemen worked hard, but nothing helped—not even the Chicago River. During the night, the wind carried sparks and pieces of burning wood across the river.

No one knows what really happened, but the O'Leary's cow has become famous for starting the Great Chicago Fire.

A City in Flames

The people of Chicago began to see that this was no ordinary fire. Soon downtown started to burn. The flames brought down grand hotels, the Tribune Building, the Federal Building, the courthouse, department stores, homes, and many other buildings.

All night and all of the next day the fire burned. At first, people tried to save some of what they owned. But the fire spread too quickly. People ran to the lake and stood in water up to their necks, afraid that they, too, might catch on fire.

> *. . . . Everybody was out of their houses, . . . and the sidewalks were covered with furniture and bundles of every description. The middle of the street was a jam of carts, carriages, wheelbarrows, and every sort of vehicle—many horses being led along, all excited and prancing, some running away. I scarcely dared look right or left, as I kept my seat by holding tightly to the trunk. The horse would not be restrained, and I had to use all my powers to keep on. I was glad to go fast, for the fire behind us raged, and the whole earth, or all we saw of it, was a lurid yellowish red.*
>
> —Mary L. Fales

The fire burned nearly everything in its path. At last the flames were put out with the help of a steady rain.

During the fire, thousands of people had taken trains out of the city. Those who had left, along with telegraph operators, spread the news of the fire. People all over the country and around the world rushed to help. Trains arrived with clothes, blankets, medicine, and food. People also sent money. Almost five million dollars came to the people of Chicago.

The damage from the fire was terrible. Almost 300 people died. Thousands were left homeless.

One person said, "A column of flame would shoot up from a burning building, catch the force of the wind, and strike the next one." Thousands of people tried to leave the city.

Up from the Ashes

"It is common to see ten or a dozen or fifty houses rising at once; but when one looks upon, not a dozen or fifty, but upon ten thousand houses rising and ten times that number of busy workmen coming and going, and listens to the noise of countless saws and hammers and chisels and axes . . ., he is bewildered."

—a man who watched Chicago being built again

Downtown Chicago and most of the north side of the city was in ashes. But all was not lost. Stockyards, grain elevators, and lumberyards on the south and west sides of the city were still working. Trains could still come into Chicago. The city's faith in itself was shown by *The Chicago Tribune*. The newspaper's office had been destroyed. From a rented space, the newspaper came out the next day. It carried a story that gave everyone hope. The message was clear. "CHEER UP! . . . CHICAGO SHALL RISE AGAIN!"

The people of Chicago wanted to make sure fire could never again destroy their city. The city council outlawed wooden buildings downtown. Right away the people set to work rebuilding. This time they would use brick and stone.

There was work for everyone. Homes, apartment buildings, schools, churches, stores, factories, train stations, and bridges had to be built. Streets had to be paved. All of the jobs brought thousands of new workers to Chicago.

A New Kind of Architecture

The fire gave young *architects* and business owners a chance to make a great name for their city. Many people who had lost their buildings built larger ones. One of these people was Potter Palmer. The new hotel he built on State Street, called the Palmer House, became world famous. Palmer also sold land on State Street to merchants who wanted to rebuild their businesses. State Street became Chicago's main shopping street.

The city also began to push upward. The need for more space downtown caused people to build taller buildings. William Jenney discovered how to make buildings extra tall—so tall that they were called skyscrapers. Jenney used a steel frame to hold them up. The steel skeleton meant the walls could be thinner and the windows bigger.

Louis Sullivan also designed skyscrapers. He combined the sleek look of the skyscraper with decoration and detail. He did not want to copy European buildings, but to create a new American architecture. Frank Lloyd Wright was one of Sullivan's students. His buildings blended with their natural surroundings. They were designed to go with the land around them. This was a new idea in architecture, and Frank Lloyd Wright is famous for it.

After the Great Chicago Fire, Marshall Field re-opened his store in a barn. Before long he was in a new building on State Street.

Frank Lloyd Wright created a style called the Prairie School.

Louis Sullivan designed this arch in 1892.

By designing the first skyscrapers, William Jenney set the stage for modern Chicago.

The Art Institute of Chicago

Chicago Culture

Even with its problems, Chicago was moving forward. It was as wealthy as many eastern cities, and the people wanted their city to have all the *culture* and art that other major cities had. We already read about the changes in architecture that were happening. People could also enjoy Chicago's culture by going to new places:

- The Art Institute of Chicago
- The Chicago Public Library
- The Chicago Symphony Orchestra
- The Chicago Opera Company

▲ Photo by Karen I. Hirsch

The World's Columbian Exposition

Less than twenty years after the fire, Chicago began preparing to hold a world's fair. Beautiful white buildings went up along the lakefront in Hyde Park. Each building was like a palace. In 1893 the fair opened. There were wonderful exhibits showing new inventions in manufacturing, transportation, art, and architecture. Many states and countries had exhibits. Women's groups displayed books written by Illinois women. They also showed inventions, weaving, ceramics, and needlework done by women. The fair was called the Columbian *Exposition* to honor Christopher Columbus' voyage to America.

People from all over the world visited the fair. They saw how new inventions could change their lives. They saw a glimpse of an exciting world to come. This was the first time electricity was used to light such a large area. Thousands of lights shining on the white buildings gave the fair the nickname "White City."

The people who planned the fair wanted to build something that would stand out above everything else. An engineer from Galesburg named George Ferris was chosen to come up with an idea. Can you guess what his idea was from his name? That's right, the Ferris wheel.

The first Ferris wheel was huge. It had thirty-six cars. It could carry more than 2,000 people. It lifted the guests high above the fairgrounds so they could see all of Chicago. A band played in one of the cars.

Have you ever been to Jackson Park in Chicago? If so, you have stood where the "Great White City" once was.

Helping Chicago's Poor

Not far from the fairgrounds, things were not as nice. Poor people still lived in crowded neighborhoods. The streets were dirty and dark. Many houses were not connected to city sewers. Often garbage was not removed.

People were coming from all around the world to live in Chicago. Immigrants came looking for work. Most of them found it. Their work was sometimes hard and dangerous. Still, it was better than being poor and jobless in their homelands.

Large numbers of immigrants came for many years. The latest group of newcomers were often the poorest people in the city. They generally lived close to downtown. They moved into neighborhoods where others from their homeland lived. There they could be around people who spoke the same language and had the same traditions as they did.

Some people tried to clean up the slums and make life better for the poor people of Chicago. One such person was Dwight L. Moody. He spent much of his life bringing religion to poor people. He liked to help children. Moody helped build the first YMCA in the country. Another such person was Jane Addams.

Jane Addams and Hull House

Jane Addams was born into a wealthy family, but from a very young age she was concerned about poor people. She was troubled by the dirty crowded slums.

On a trip to England Jane saw something called a settlement house. It was a place for the poor to live that was clean and safe. When she got home she made a plan. She would move to Chicago and start a settlement house there. The settlement house would offer all kinds of help to people in need.

Jane and her college friend, Ellen Starr, went to churches, *charities*, and rich people to get money for their project. They found a rundown mansion in a poor area of Chicago. The mansion had once been the home of a wealthy man named Charles J. Hull. Jane Addams bought the mansion, fixed it up, and moved in. She named the new settlement house Hull House.

In the first year over 50,000 visitors came. At Hull House Addams and Starr started a kindergarten. They also started clubs for children and adults. Hull House was a place for people to meet and enjoy themselves. They could learn to sing or just talk with their neighbors. Many immigrants took classes in English, child care, art, cooking, and sewing. Hull House made Chicago a happier place for newcomers. The idea caught on. People started settlement houses all over the country.

ILLINOIS PORTRAIT

Jane Addams
1860–1935

Jane Addams reads to children at Hull House, which she founded in 1889.

Jane Addams was born in Cedarville, Illinois. As Jane grew up she visited sewing schools for poor children and homes for the elderly. She was very concerned about the poor. She believed that to really understand how to help the poor, she should live among them. She moved to Chicago and started Hull House, the first settlement house in Chicago. It helped thousands of people. Jane Addams worked very hard all over the world to help people and support peace. She worked to get women the right to vote. She helped start the American Civil Liberties Union. In 1931 she became the first woman to win the Nobel Peace Prize.

The "El" Train

In the late 1800s a company came up with a plan to build an above-the-street railroad in downtown Chicago. They thought this was a good idea because street traffic (horse and buggy traffic, that is) was getting too crowded.

The above-the-street railroads are called **elevated** railroads. Some people call them the "elevated." In Chicago most people simply call this system the "El." At first, elevated trains ran on steam. Later they used electricity.

People today use the El to get around the city quickly. They may take it to work, to go shopping, or for lots of other reasons. The El in the part of Chicago called the Loop is famous. It has been shown in movies and television shows.

The Loop got its name when streetcar tracks were built in a circle around downtown in the 1880s.

The Addison Street El stop is by Wrigley Field, home of the Chicago Cubs. Many Cubs fans take the El to the games to avoid traffic jams and parking problems.

The River that Flows Backwards

In the 1880s and 1890s many Chicago children became ill. Some of them died. The trouble was the city's drinking water. Chicago got its drinking water from Lake Michigan. After heavy rains, city waste ran into the Chicago River. Then the river carried it into the lake. As the city grew, it became very hard to keep the lake water near Chicago clean enough to drink. Something had to be done.

An enormous project was proposed. What if the flow of the Chicago River could be reversed? Then the polluted water would flow away from Lake Michigan. A canal had to be built to make this happen. It was called the Chicago Sanitary and Ship Canal. For eight years Chicagoans worked to dig the canal. Thousands of immigrants helped.

The canal helped the pollution problem. It also connected the Chicago River to the Des Plaines River. The canal would be used by boats going between Lake Michigan and the Mississippi River.

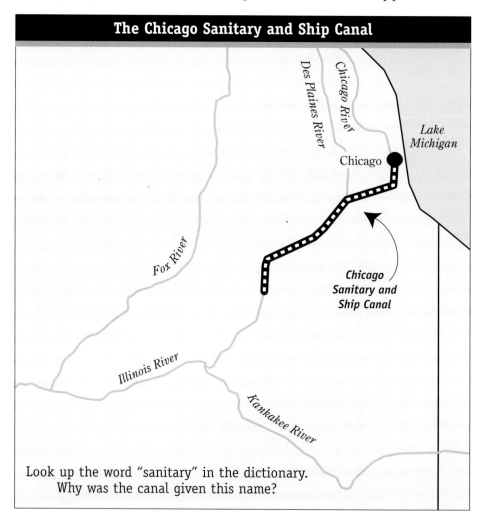

The Chicago Sanitary and Ship Canal

Look up the word "sanitary" in the dictionary. Why was the canal given this name?

Chicago Today

Today the stockyards are gone and the goods in Marshall Field's department store have changed. Chicago is home to modern industries such as processed foods, household appliances, railroad equipment, telephone equipment, printing, chemicals, plastics, paints, cleaning solutions, and many more.

The Sears Tower is the tallest building in the world. It was built in 1973.

In Chicago today you can find older style buildings, like the Wrigley Building, and modern skyscrapers, like the Prudential Building.

A man on stilts creates balloon figures at Navy Pier.

The Field Museum of Natural History was started by Marshall Field. This is how it looks today.

Go Chicago!

Are you a Bulls fan? A Cubs fan? A White Sox fan? A Bears fan? A Blackhawks fan?

Chicago sports teams bring the community together. They also bring a lot of money to our state.

Many fans come to Wrigley Field to watch the Cubs play.

Ethnic Groups

How many *ethnic* groups are there in Chicago? Well, how many are there in the United States? The lists are about the same.

Chicago's people are Native American, African American, Chinese, German, Irish, Scottish, English, Swedish, Norwegian, Asian, Hispanic, Czech, Lithuanian, Latvian, Ukrainian, Polish, Jewish, Italian, Greek, and the list goes on.

Immigrants have been coming to Chicago for over a hundred years. But did you know that nearly half of the foreign-born people living in Chicago today came just in the last twenty years? Chicago is still an attractive place to live the American dream.

Ethnic neighborhoods have grown up where groups of immigrants settled. You can visit many different cultures by visiting these neighborhoods. The people celebrate their traditions with festivals and events.

These are some of the many faces of Chicago.

In Chicago today, the two most common languages spoken at home (other than English) are Spanish and Polish.

A Changing City, A Changing State

Chicago is a case study of what was happening to much of Illinois. Our state was growing and changing. Every change seemed to bring about more changes. People were changing the way they traveled. They changed the way they farmed. They changed the way they built buildings and the way they made products. Chicagoans had never lived during a time with so much change. But it was just the beginning. The twentieth century was just around the corner. It was about to take Chicagoans, and everyone in Illinois, on a roller coaster ride of changes.

activity

Compare and Contrast Catalogs
When people lived a long way from stores, they often shopped
by mail. They sent their orders and their money to catalogs.
Here are some items that were sold in early catalogs:
- oil lamps
- ice boxes
- horse harnesses
- wagon wheels
- horse-drawn plows
- clothes for men, women, and children

1. Do people still shop by mail today? What catalogs have
   you seen?

2. What things have taken the place of these items in today's
   catalogs?

Questions for Review

1. Who is the founder of Chicago? (Hint: He started a trading post.)

2. Why was Chicago such a good place to do business?

3. What are stockyards?

4. Who started the first department store? Who made mail-order catalogs popular?

5. Why did workers go on strike?

6. How did George Pullman try to keep his workers happy? Did it work?

7. How did the Great Chicago Fire start?

8. Who designed the first skyscraper?

9. What was the World's Columbian Exposition?

10. How did the city solve the problem of polluted drinking water?

Geography Tie-In

1. Why did Chicago's location make it such a good place for settlement? For industry?

2. Where is your town located (if not in Chicago)? How does its location influence the
   way people live?

THE TIME
1880–1940

PEOPLE TO KNOW
Charles Duryea
Hieronymus Mueller
Dr. James Selkirk
Walt Disney
Louis Armstrong
Duke Ellington
Benny Goodman
Red Grange
Robert Abbott
Al Capone
Eugene Williams
Joe Leiter

PLACES TO LOCATE
Poland
Austria
Germany
Russia
Italy
Greece
China
Japan
Mexico
Southeast Asia
Springfield
Decatur
England
France
Chicago
Zeigler

timeline of events

1880–1910
Immigrants
pour into the
United States
and Illinois.

1905
Robert Abbott
starts a weekly
newspaper called the
Chicago Defender.

1880   1890   1900

1893
Charles and Frank
Duryea make the first
gasoline-powered
automobile.

1896
Duryea cars
are sold to
the public.

1901
Walt Disney, the
creator of Mickey
Mouse, is born in
Chicago.

chapter 10

A New Century

TERMS TO UNDERSTAND
famine
tradition
tenement
seamstress
discrimination
resident
advancement
generator
animated
civilian
military
consumer
rural
urban
prohibit
prosperity
credit
stock

Charles Duryea of Illinois built the first gasoline-powered automobile in the United States. Automobiles changed the style of life for people in the new century.

1913 Illinois women win the right to vote. Henry Ford makes automobiles using an assembly line.

1914 Black musicians bring jazz to Chicago.

1915 The Great Migration of black people from the South begins.

1919–1933
Liquor is banned in the United States.

1910	1920	1930	1940

1909
The NAACP is founded after a race riot in Springfield.

1914–1918
World War I
—
The U.S. enters World War I in 1917.

1920
The first radio station goes on the air.

1920s
Roaring Twenties

1929
The stock market crashes.

1927
The first talking movie, *The Jazz Singer*, is released.

1930s
Great Depression

**Top Five Reasons
People Come to America**

1. To escape poverty and poor living conditions

2. To enjoy the freedoms of *democracy*

3. To escape war

4. To practice the religion of their choice

5. To join other family members

A century is a period of 100 years.

A Time of Change

We have seen how Illinois changed during the nineteenth century. It would change even more during the next 100 years. As the new century began, immigrants poured into the state and cities grew. The country went to war. People in Illinois and all across the United States faced good times and bad times.

Immigration

At the beginning of the twentieth century, millions of immigrants were coming to our country. Why would so many people leave their homes and families and risk a dangerous trip across the ocean?

The people who came here were looking for a better life. Some who came were looking for a place where they could be free to follow their own religious beliefs. Others left their homelands because of war. Some came because in America there was land and the promise of jobs. Some immigrants had to leave their countries simply to survive. In Ireland there was a *famine*. People were starving. Russian, Polish, and German Jews left because the government was driving them out. People throughout Europe had heard stories about America. They called it the "land of opportunity."

At first, most immigrants came from England, Ireland, Germany, and Sweden. Soon new groups joined them. Poles, Austrians, Bohemians, Russians, Jews, Italians, Greeks, and Romanians came. For the most part they settled in Chicago, Rockford, Aurora, Joliet, and Elgin. In these cities the newcomers could find work in factories. Chinese and Japanese people came from Asia. Mexicans also came hoping to find work.

These English emigrants are about to get on a ship to come to America.

By Foot, by Boat, by Train They Came

No matter what country they came from, the people had a long journey ahead of them. Just to leave their homelands they had to walk great distances or take trains to get to the nearest port. Then they often had to wait days or weeks for the next ship. On the ship there was not much to eat. Many people were seasick. The ships moved slowly, taking several months to reach America.

Often the journey did not end when the ships reached America. Many immigrants still had to travel to places like Illinois. When they arrived, they usually settled in cities and neighborhoods that were already filled with people from their homeland. There they could speak the language of their home country. They could keep their *traditions*.

After landing in America, immigrants were registered at Ellis Island in New York. Those moving on to Illinois still had a long journey ahead of them.

Vincenza Lange was just five years old when she came from Italy to America. She was afraid to sign up for school because she didn't speak English very well. A family friend who spoke English took her to school. When the teacher asked the shy girl her name, she mumbled "Vincenza." The teacher was confused and wrote down her name as something else. From then on she was known as "Jessica."

Struggling in a New Land

Immigrants helped build railroads and canals. They started farms, stores, and businesses. By 1900 they were working in steel mills, farm machinery factories, and meat-packing plants.

The people worked long hard hours. For all their work they were paid very low wages. The wages were so low that often the women and children in a family had to go to work so there would be enough money for food and rent.

There were no laws to protect workers. As a result, people often worked in terrible and dangerous conditions.

Life at home often wasn't much better. Most immigrants lived in *tenement* buildings or in dark basement apartments. They were often dirty and shabby.

Mary Carpenter came from Hungary when she was seventeen years old. She came on the ship *Carpathia*. It was the ship that picked up the *Titanic* survivors on a later trip. Mary was the only one of her family to come, and she was very homesick. She could not call home or send e-mail like we can today. She could only write letters, and they took months to reach a European village.

Some immigrants returned to their homelands, but for many, the problems in America were still better than returning to the old country.

Papa said that it was no longer safe for a Jewish family in Russia, so we are going to America. . . . Papa and mama are busy selling most of our belongings. Mama told me and my little sister, Ana, to each pick one book and one toy to bring with us. Ana cried. She's only four. But I'm ten and must be brave and reasonable, Mama says.
—Alvin Sandrovitch

These immigrants are waiting for a train.
Can you see the trunks, bags, and crates full of their belongings?

Cities and Industries Grow

Once Illinois was a state of farms and small towns. More and more it was becoming a state of larger towns and cities. By the 1920s many people in Illinois lived in cities.

More people went to work in factories. Illinois factories made all kinds of products. People also worked in offices and businesses. They sold things in department stores, drug stores, and grocery stores.

The growth of cities and industries caused many problems. People saw many things that needed to be changed. Poverty, child labor, long working hours, dangerous workplaces, dirty streets, unsafe water and food, no garbage collection, and no street cleaning were growing problems. People began to think about what to do to solve them.

Linking the past and the present

In the early 1900s many of Illinois' new workers were women. They started leaving their homes to get jobs. They were teachers, nurses, secretaries, *seamstresses*, and store clerks.

Today women also work at many other jobs. Women are doctors, lawyers, truck drivers, basketball players, engineers, business managers, repair people, electricians, and computer programmers. Illinois women work at every kind of job there is.

Here are some things that people did to solve the problems at home and at work. They passed laws so that:

• Children under the age of fourteen could not work in mines.

• Workers could not be fired for joining a labor union.

• Bosses had to pay their workers no less than a certain amount of money.

• Mines had to have rules for safety.

• Workers hurt on the job could still get paid.

• Milk sold in stores would have to be clean and fresh.

• Companies could not pollute the air and water.

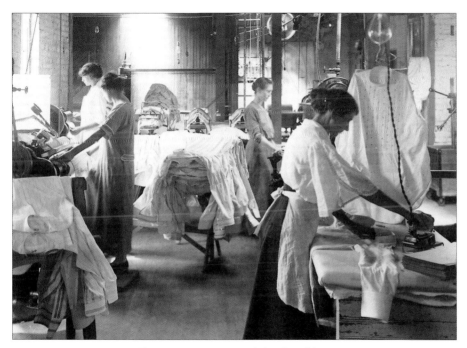

These women are at work ironing shirts.

• Cities would collect garbage regularly.

• Cities would put in the sewer systems needed for indoor bathrooms. At that time most people still had outhouses.

Discrimination

One problem that wasn't solved so easily was *discrimination*. Many white people did not give black people a chance just because of their race. It was a difficult time for blacks all over the country. They were treated unfairly. They were not allowed in movie theaters or clubs. Most restaurants would not let them sit with everybody else. Public places had separate bathrooms and drinking fountains for blacks.

In 1908 in the town of Springfield, white people tried to remove black *residents*. This caused a riot in the town. The next year, a group of people, both black and white, met in New York to try to stop the unfair treatment of black people. They started a group called the National Association for the *Advancement* of Colored People (NAACP). They planned to talk to people in Congress about making laws to end discrimination. They also planned to travel around the country teaching people to respect the rights of black people.

ILLINOIS PORTRAIT

Walt Disney
1901–1966

The creator of Mickey Mouse and Donald Duck was born in Chicago. After studying art, he drew cartoons for advertisements. When Disney was twenty-one he moved to California. He wanted to work in the new movie business. He and his brother Roy began making *animated* cartoons. Mickey Mouse first appeared in a cartoon called *Steamboat Willie*. Walt Disney was the first person to make a movie-length cartoon. He used up all of his savings to make it, not knowing if it would be a hit. It was called *Snow White and the Seven Dwarfs* and it was indeed a hit. In 1955 another dream of Disney's came true. Disneyland opened in California.

Inventions Make Life Easier

Electricity

Many inventions changed people's lives. Electric *generators* were one of the most important. They changed the way people worked, played, and lived.

Generators are machines for making electricity. They made electric lights possible. Electric streetcars ran through cities and towns. New machines that used electricity were invented. There were electric washing machines, irons, stoves, refrigerators, and vacuum cleaners.

Telephones

Alexander Graham Bell, who had invented the telephone many years before, talked on the line from coast to coast. People in Illinois could make local calls before 1900, but it took another thirty years before nearly all homes and businesses had phone service.

Radio and Moving Pictures

Two of the most exciting inventions were the radio and the movies. Everyone across the United States wanted a radio. At first there were not enough to go around. People visited friends who were lucky enough to own one. They gathered around to listen to their favorite programs. They were amazed. Imagine hearing voices and music that came from the air!

The first movies were silent, with no talking. Then movie makers figured out how to add sound. The new "talkies" were a hit. A movie cost twenty-five cents for adults and ten cents for children. At first movie theaters were small, but soon large fancy theaters were built.

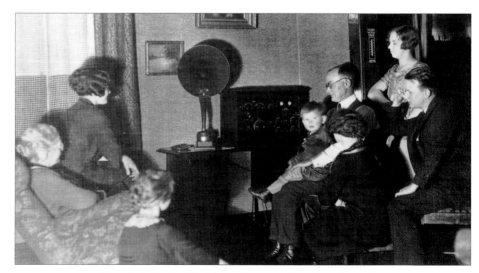

The whole family liked to gather around to hear the radio.

Automobiles

After 1920 automobiles became very popular. For $400, a person could own a Ford. The price was reasonable, and many people bought them. Henry Ford owned the factory that made Ford cars. He joked that people could have any color car they wanted, as long as it was black.

Most roads were just paths made of dirt. When the weather was dry, people choked on the dust. When it rained, horses had to pull the cars through the mud. Then Illinois started to build new and better roads. They raised the money for the new roads by putting a small tax on gasoline.

People from Illinois tried to build cars. Hieronymus Mueller of Decatur was one of the first. But his effort ended in disaster. He was killed in an explosion while building his "Mueller" car. One hundred car companies went into business at different places in Illinois. None of them lasted very long. Dr. James Selkirk, of Aurora, built only one car.

Changing Times, Changing Needs

Before automobiles, horses and mules and other work animals were used for transportation. Horses were kept in stables. Stable owners fed them, brushed them, and provided them with stalls to sleep in. Blacksmith shops made horseshoes. Other shops made and sold saddles, harnesses, and wagons. With the coming of the automobile, those businesses were not needed as much. New ones were needed. What were some of them?

Can you think of other things that changed because of the automobile? Here are some hints: vacations, jobs, land alongside the roads, movement of products, and even sports.

Some people did not like the new "horseless carriage."
As drivers cruised by, people sometimes shouted, "Get a horse!"

World War I

Soon after the new century began, a war started. The fighting involved so many countries that it was called a "world war." On one side were the Central Powers. They included Germany and Austria-Hungary. On the other side were England, France, Russia, and the United States. They were the Allied Powers. World War I claimed the lives of ten million people.

Joining the Allies

When the war started in Europe, the United States wanted to stay out of it. But then something happened that made them get involved. German submarines sank American ships. After that, the United States joined the Allies.

People who were not soldiers helped by buying war bonds. This gave the government money to use to pay for the war. After the war, the people could trade in their war bonds for more money.

Boys from the cities helped farmers harvest their crops. Women made hospital supplies at Red Cross centers. They learned to cook without wheat or meat so these foods could be sent to Europe.

Since the war was fought in Europe, many farms there were destroyed. *Civilians* as well as soldiers needed food and other farm products. Illinois farmers stepped up to help. They sent some of their crops overseas.

Many tanks and weapons were made in Illinois factories. In fact, one in every three items made in Illinois went toward winning the war.

Illinois Does Its Part

Men from all over the United States came to Illinois to train to be soldiers. They trained at Camp Grant near Rockford. At the Great Lakes Naval Training Station near Chicago they became sailors. They learned to fly airplanes at bases near Belleville and Rantoul. Illinois supplied 300,000 people for **military** duty.

Rockford
Chicago
Rantoul
Belleville

Rockford
Chicago
Moline
Rock Island
Joliet
Peoria
Alton
East St. Louis

- Steel was produced in Joliet and Chicago Heights.
- Peoria factories made farm equipment and steel wire.
- East St. Louis was a leader in making aluminum and animal feeds.
- Rockford and Moline factories made parts for machines.
- Alton manufactured brass for bullets.
- Guns were tested and stored at Rock Island.

Some women joined the Illinois Drum and Bugle Corps in World War I.

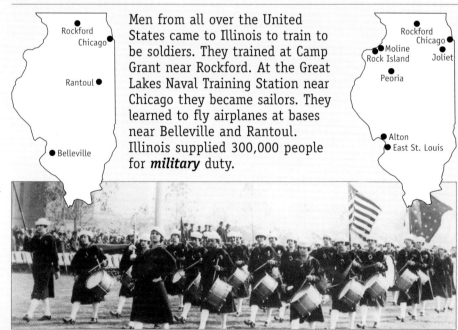

The Roaring Twenties

As the war ended, Americans returned from Europe. They wanted to forget the war. People who had lived with shortages wanted to live well. Factories switched from making war materials to making goods for *consumers*. People wanted to buy the new products they saw in store windows.

People worked hard but they also looked for ways to have fun. There were goldfish-swallowing contests and marathon dances. Couples danced a new dance called the Charleston. For the first time in America, women cut their hair short and wore shorter dresses.

People bought new products like radios and refrigerators. They listened to the new sounds of jazz by Louis Armstrong, Benny Goodman, Duke Ellington, and Jelly Roll Morton. For the first time people went to sporting events in large numbers. Athletes such as Red Grange, the "galloping ghost" of the Chicago Bears, became heroes. The 1920s became known as the Roaring Twenties.

The Great Migration

At the beginning of the new century, most African Americans lived in *rural* areas in the South. Then black people from the South began to move north to find better jobs. They also wanted to escape racial violence in the South. Soon thousands of black people were moving north to Chicago, where there were more opportunities. Most lived in *urban* areas. This movement north to the cities is known as the Great Migration.

A newspaper called the *Chicago Defender* encouraged blacks to move to Chicago. It listed names of churches and people they could write to for help. The Bethlehem Baptist Association in Chicago helped many black families find housing and work. Many who came had to work for other people for low wages. Some started businesses. Ernest Morris opened the "Perfect Eat" Shop on 47th Street near South Park.

Gangsters and Bootleg Gin

The 1920s were also a time of crime and violence. One reason was because of liquor. In 1919 liquor was outlawed in the United States. Those who still wanted to drink went to "speakeasies," or clubs where they could buy liquor. The liquor was supplied by gangsters such as Al Capone. "Bootlegging" (secretly buying and selling liquor) became big business.

The liquor law was called Prohibition, because it prohibited the sale of alcohol. The law did not last long. Liquor was made legal again in 1933.

ILLINOIS PORTRAIT

Robert S. Abbott
1868–1940

Robert Abbott started a weekly newspaper called the *Chicago Defender*. He had graduated from the Kent School of Law in Chicago, but he was not allowed to practice law because he was black. Abbott decided to use his skills in another way. He started publishing the *Chicago Defender* with just $25 and a typewriter. Abbott's newspaper was one of the first African American newspapers in the country to have over 100,000 readers. It influenced thousands of black people to move to Chicago. Abbott's nephew, John H. Sengstacke, started the *Chicago Daily Defender*. He wanted to "improve the quality of life" for all Americans. His paper became the largest African American daily paper in the country.

Chicago Blues and Jazz

Today, Chicago has many blues festivals to celebrate this art form.

▲ Photo by John D. Ivanko

The Blues

When black people moved north they brought a new kind of music. The blues is a type of music that comes from old slave songs. Usually the songs are about sadness, lost love, problems with money, or other hardships. Most of the time a man or woman sings to the music of a guitar. Today we use the phrase "singin' the blues" to mean feeling sad. Have you ever "sung the blues"?

African American music grew quickly after the slaves were freed. The blues found its way to Chicago and became popular there. Famous blues musicians include B.B. King, Koko Taylor, and Bessie Smith. The rock and soul music we hear today has its roots in the blues.

Jazz

Like the blues, jazz music began in the South, in New Orleans. Blues songs and African American folk music developed into a new art form. It had a new kind of rhythm, and some of the notes were played off beat. Band members improvised, or made up melodies as they went along. The new modern art form was called jazz.

Many jazz players were moving north. There were better jobs in northern cities such as Chicago and New York. Chicago became famous for its jazz. Chicago jazz came from the New Orleans style but it had more solos and more complicated rhythms.

Jazz musicians such as Bud Freeman, Benny Goodman, Joe "King" Oliver, and Louis Armstrong played jazz in Chicago. The 1920s became known as the Jazz Age.

Benny Goodman

The Original Creole Orchestra arrived in Chicago in 1914. They started the South Side of Chicago swinging with the sounds of jazz. Soon other bands were formed and jazz clubs opened around the city.

Louis Armstrong
1900-1971

Louis Armstrong was born in New Orleans, where jazz music was born. His grandparents had been slaves. His family was very poor. His father Willie worked in a turpentine plant. His mother Mary Ann worked as a housekeeper. When Louis was thirteen years old he learned to play a bugle. Later he earned money by singing on the street. Then he joined a Mississippi riverboat band.

In 1922 Louis Armstrong came to Chicago to play in King Oliver's Creole Jazz Band. He played the trumpet and started a great career in jazz and swing music. He became the first great jazz trumpeter. He helped to make Chicago the second most important place for jazz in the United States.

Trouble on the Homefront

While the end of the war brought happiness and *prosperity*, it also brought problems. Many African Americans had served in the war. After helping America win, they expected a warm welcome home. Instead, they found that prejudice had not gone away. Life at home had not changed very much.

While the war was on, many blacks had moved north for jobs in factories and mines. When white soldiers came home from the war, they could not find jobs. They blamed the black workers for taking all the jobs. Strong feelings of anger between blacks and whites grew.

Eventually, racial prejudice exploded into violence. A riot broke out in East St. Louis. White and black mobs attacked one another. More than forty black people were killed. Thousands were chased from their homes.

Just a few years later, riots took place in other cities and towns in the United States. One of the worst came in July of 1919. Eugene Williams was swimming in Lake Michigan. White swimmers did not like where he was swimming. They said he was in water that was reserved for whites. Arguments broke out and people began throwing stones at each another. Williams could not come out of the water. He hung on to a piece of wood as long as he could. Finally, he could not hang on any longer. He drowned.

Rumors spread that Williams had been stoned to death. Five days of rioting between blacks and whites followed. Soldiers had to be called in to stop the fighting. Twenty-three blacks and fifteen whites were killed in the battles. Hundreds of people were hurt.

The Miners' Struggle

After the war some workers were unhappy again. Industries had done well during the war. Workers wanted to share in their success. They wanted higher wages. They wanted safer working conditions. Workers and owners struggled with each other. Coal mining was a good example of this struggle.

Ninety million tons of coal were mined in Illinois in 1918. The coal miners worked long hours. The mines were dangerous and dirty. Even so, the job only paid a few dollars a day.

Miners thought a union might be the answer. But the mine owners did not want unions. When workers tried to start unions, tempers flared. Soon a "war" was underway between coal miners and mine owners. It lasted for thirty years.

One of the biggest coal wars took place at the Leiter mine near Zeigler. Joe Leiter had bought a coal mine in Franklin County. He also built a town for his workers. His mine became the largest in Illinois.

Leiter's miners wanted the company to recognize their union. They wanted to be paid the same as miners working nearby. They wanted only members of their union to work in the Leiter mine. The company said no, so the workers went on strike.

Without workers, Leiter could not mine coal. He hired black miners from the South to come to Illinois. He also hired immigrants from Europe. As the new workers arrived, they were met by angry men on strike. The strikers yelled and even shot at the new workers. Many of them fled, but some stayed and worked.

The Great Depression

A depression is a time when most people can't make enough money to take care of their families. They want to work, but they can't find jobs. The depression of the 1930s was the worst depression the United States has ever known. That is why it is called the Great Depression.

Farmers felt the depression first. After World War I American farmers continued to harvest record crops. With large amounts of farm products and fewer buyers, prices went down. Farmers who had borrowed money to buy equipment and seed couldn't pay their bills. Many lost their farms.

People stopped buying things such as radios, cars, and washing machines. That left stores with goods they couldn't sell. Factories did not need to produce as much so they sent workers home. Without paychecks, workers couldn't spend as much as they had before. More businesses slowed down. People without work couldn't pay for things they had bought on *credit*. Banks couldn't pay for *stocks* they bought. Then the stock market crashed. The price of stocks went so low that banks and other people who bought stocks lost large amounts of money. Banks closed because they ran out of money. People lost their life savings.

Men sold apples on street corners to earn money. People stood in long lines to get soup and bread handouts. They grew gardens in their backyards. They saved everything they could. They mended old clothes again and again to make them last longer. When people had worn holes in the bottoms of their shoes, they put cardboard inside.

In one school, a teacher asked a girl, "What's wrong with you?"

"I'm just hungry," the girl said.

"You may go home and eat," the teacher said.

"I can't," the child answered. "Today is my sister's turn to eat."

Leiter knew he was in trouble. He could not run his mine without experienced miners. He was also in trouble for not following Illinois' mine safety laws. Leiter did about the only thing he could. He sold his mine.

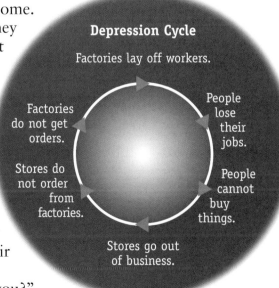

Depression Cycle

Factories lay off workers.

People lose their jobs.

People cannot buy things.

Stores go out of business.

Stores do not order from factories.

Factories do not get orders.

> "I did what I had to do. I always seemed to find a way to make things work. We just did what we had to do, just one day at a time."
>
> —a young mother during the depression

These Chicago men are looking for work during the Great Depression. Can you read their qualifications on their signs?

Starved Rock Lodge and Conference Center was built by the CCC in the 1930s. Since then it has been remodeled. Visitors can stay in guest rooms or cabins. They can swim, hike, ride horses, and much more.

The New Deal

The government decided to take action. President Franklin Roosevelt wanted people to start working again. He had a plan. He called his plan the New Deal, because it would give Americans a "new deal of the cards." He started projects in order to create jobs. The government hired people to build dams, repair highways, build new courthouses and schools, and fix up parks. The government loaned farmers money so they could stay in business. Young people were trained for jobs. Children got free school lunches. Older people got money called Social Security.

One of the new programs was the Civilian Conservation Corps (CCC). The CCC put men to work in state parks across America. One of these was Starved Rock State Park in Illinois. The workers built the Starved Rock Lodge and Conference Center.

activity

Graphs Tell an Interesting Story

Use the graphs to answer the questions.

1. Did the number of people living on farms go up or down from 1910 to 1970?

2. Were more people living on farms in 1870 or one hundred years later?

3. How much money did farm goods bring in 1890?

4. How much money did farm goods bring in 1930?

5. Did the money made from other goods rise or fall from 1890 to 1930?

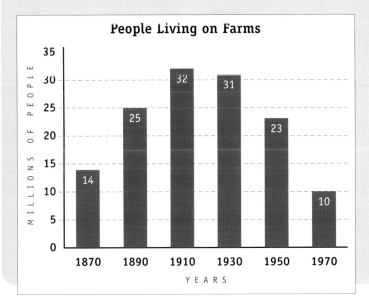

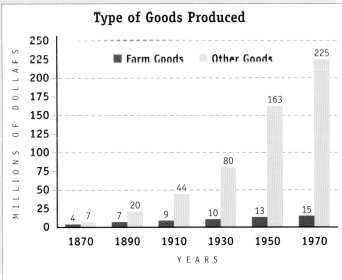

Questions for Review

1. List three reasons why immigrants came to America.

2. Describe the journey an immigrant had to make from Europe to Illinois.

3. List three inventions that changed the style of life in the new century.

4. How did Illinois help the country in World War I?

5. What was the Great Migration?

6. What made life difficult for black people during this time?

7. List some of the things people did for fun in the Roaring Twenties.

8. How did the Great Depression affect farmers?

9. How did President Roosevelt put people back to work?

Taking Our Place in the World

THE TIME
1940–2000

PEOPLE TO KNOW
President Franklin D.
    Roosevelt
Arthur Compton
"Baby Boomers"
Dr. Martin Luther King Jr.
Ernest Hemingway
Carl Sandburg
Gwendolyn Brooks
Jane Byrne
Harold Washington
Ronald Reagan

PLACES TO LOCATE
Pearl Harbor, Hawaii
Japan
Cicero
Seneca
University of Chicago

World War II pilots examine their plane after an accident
at Chanute Training Field in central Illinois.

timeline of events

1941
December 7
The Japanese bomb
Pearl Harbor,
Hawaii.

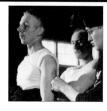

1950–1953
Korean War

1955
Richard Daley begins
twenty years as mayor
of Chicago.

1940   1950   1960

1939–1945
World War II

1941
The U.S. enters World War II.

1950s
The "Baby Boomers"
start families and move
to the suburbs.

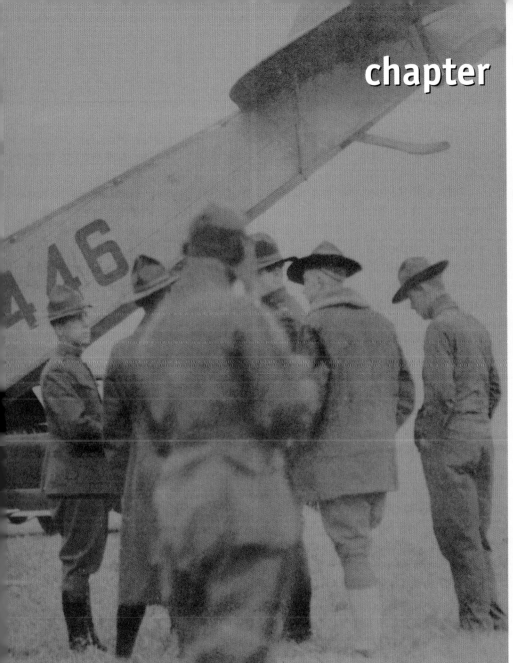

chapter

11

1966 Dr. Martin Luther King Jr. visits Chicago.

1968 Dr. King is murdered.

1975
Video cassette recorders (VCRs)
are first sold to the public.

1986
Three out of five
families own
microwave ovens.

1990s
More and more people
buy personal computers for
their homes.

1970

1980

1990

2000

1963–1975
Vietnam War

1970
Illinois'
constitution
is updated.

1979
Jane Byrne
becomes the
first female
mayor of
Chicago.

1983
Harold Washington
becomes the first
black mayor of
Chicago.

1993
The Upper Mississippi
River floods.

1960s
Civil Rights Movement

1990s
Illinois' Hispanic and Asian
communities grow.

Men entering the navy had to have shots before they went overseas to fight in World War II.

The town of Seneca made huge ships for planes to land on. Seneca became known as the "Prairie Shipyard." The huge ships were floated down the Illinois and Mississippi Rivers to the ocean for use in the war.

Seneca ●

A Second World War

President Roosevelt's New Deal was helping to end the Great Depression. Then something happened that ended the depression for good—a war.

In 1939 a second world war began in Europe. The United States did not get involved for the first two years. It entered the war after a surprise attack on Pearl Harbor, Hawaii. Japanese submarines and planes bombed a U.S. naval base there. Nearly 3,000 people were killed or wounded, and many American ships and planes were destroyed. The next day President Roosevelt asked for a declaration of war. The U.S. joined the Allied Powers.

Illinois Helps in the Cause

Illinois was a leader in the war effort. One million people from Illinois joined the armed forces. They were trained, along with other Americans, at bases such as Great Lakes Naval Air Base and Camp Grant. Because a large army had to be trained quickly, hotels and parks in Chicago were turned into *barracks* and training fields. Chicago also opened an officers' club for servicemen and servicewomen.

At the time, black soldiers were separated from white soldiers. They had little chance to move up in the army. Illinois tried to fix this problem by building an all-black training camp, Camp Robert Smalls. Camp Smalls helped black soldiers learn skills that would help them not only in the war but after they returned home.

Women were not trained for *combat*, but they served as nurses, instructors, office workers, photographers, and electronics specialists. Some women were trained as pilots.

Illinois' factories and farms went into high gear. The largest factory in the world was built in Chicago to make airplane engines. Huge plants opened in Rockford, Rock Island, Peoria, Springfield, Decatur, and East St. Louis. Illinois even made boats for the navy. The Western Electric Company in Cicero made *radar* equipment. A plant near Kankakee made over one billion pounds of explosives. The Pullman Company made tanks and airplane parts.

Farms produced record crops. Illinois led the nation in soybeans. It was second in cheese, hogs, and corn. Illinois farmers used seed and fertilizer in the rich prairie soil. The combination helped them grow food for Americans at home and soldiers at war.

Help from Home

People who stayed at home did their part. It was hard to get such things as coffee, nylon stockings, and alarm clocks. The materials that went into making those items were being used to make bullets, parachutes, and other war goods. Some goods were sent to the soldiers overseas. If the people complained, storekeepers answered, "Don't you know there's a war on?"

One way to save things that were scarce was to *ration* them. This meant people could buy only so much sugar, meat, butter, coffee, gas, and tires. Each family was given ration stamps every month to buy these things. When their stamps ran out, they could not buy the items until the next month when they would get more stamps.

People tried to make things last. They planted "victory gardens" to grow their own vegetables, so they would not need to buy them from the store.

More women went to work for wages outside the home. Many of them worked at jobs men used to do. People found out that women are good aircraft mechanics, welders, truck drivers, and carpenters.

Children also did their part. They collected pots, pans, and tin cans that could be turned into metal for making ships.

Ration coupons had to be used to buy certain things at the store. This one belonged to Beth Gerrard Allen. Her husband, brother, and brothers-in-law were in the air force. At her job, she helped repair airplanes that would be sent overseas for the war.

Many workers were needed during the war. Some teenagers were allowed to quit school and go to work in factories.

Women went to work to help the war effort. This picture was taken in 1943.

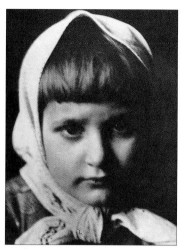

A young Jewish girl wrote: "Next year would have been my last year at school, but I won't be able to graduate . . . the schools have closed. . . . The Nazis have forced more than 5,000 Jews in Minsk . . . to live in one small area of the town."

Scientist Arthur Compton directed the research for the bomb. He won a Nobel Prize in physics. He had to keep the experiments at Stagg Field on the University of Chicago campus top secret.

The Holocaust

Millions of soldiers and civilians died during World War II. That didn't include the death of six million Jews. These people didn't lose their lives fighting as soldiers or living in a city that was bombed. They were murdered. They died for one reason only—because they were Jewish. This mass murder is called the *Holocaust*.

When Adolf Hitler became the leader of Germany, he made one law after another that took rights away from Jewish people. They were forced out of their jobs. Their own country said they were no longer citizens. Many Jews fled Germany, but most stayed. They thought that, as Germans, they would be safe. They were wrong.

Jewish *synagogues* were destroyed. Everything they owned was taken away. Jews were loaded onto trains. Family members were separated. Many never saw each other again. After rounding up Jews from several European countries, Hitler had them sent to concentration camps. At the camps, millions of Jews were killed. Those who weren't killed were treated horribly. There was hardly anything to eat and no way to keep warm.

When the war ended, U.S. soldiers went to free the people in the concentration camps. They were shocked and horrified at what they found. The survivors looked like walking skeletons.

The damage to the Jewish people was too enormous ever to be repaired. Entire families were wiped out. Survivors spent lifetimes looking for lost relatives.

The Atomic Bomb

During the war, countries on both sides tried to build a super bomb. The United States and Great Britain finished the bomb first. They won the race when scientists figured out how to split the atom. The scientists were working at the University of Chicago. To be sure their ideas worked, they did an experiment. Under the stands of the football field, they split an atom for the first time. They could now produce a new form of energy called *atomic* energy. That energy was used in two bombs that finally ended World War II.

A Booming State and Nation

The war was over. Americans came back home wanting to start living again. Our country was grateful for their sacrifices. The government passed a law that would help soldiers who had gone to war pay for their education. It was called the GI Bill. Thousands of ex-soldiers went to colleges and trade schools in Illinois. They were also able to get loans to buy homes and start businesses.

Economic Boom

People had little to spend their money on during the war. Factories were busy making goods to help win the war. That changed when the war ended. Factories started making consumer goods again. They made refrigerators, stoves, washing machines, furniture, televisions, radios, and lawn mowers. Fast food restaurant chains also started at this time. The original McDonald's Restaurant opened in Des Plaines. (Their national headquarters and training center are in Oak Brook.) Before long McDonald's could be found from coast to coast.

People also spent money on music. They bought thousands of phonographs (record players). The most popular music was something new called rock and roll. Everyone wanted records by Bo Diddley, Jerry Lee Lewis, the Supremes, and Elvis Presley.

Baby Boom

The world was at peace and the future seemed safe. There seemed to be jobs for everyone. Families started having more babies. That's why adults in their fifties and sixties today are called "Baby Boomers."

Larger families bought more goods. They needed clothes, diapers, food, furniture, and bigger houses. Most of all, it seems they wanted automobiles.

Advertisements told families that cars were necessary. Cars could take people to work and into the country on vacations. The ads also changed people's minds about how many cars one family needed. One car was enough for work. But a second car was also necessary, they said, to take children to school and pick up groceries.

With all the new cars came new roads and highways. President Dwight Eisenhower signed a bill that created a new kind of highway. It was called the interstate. Interstates connected one state with another. In times of war they would be used to move troops and supplies. At all other times Americans could use the roads for business and recreation.

Today the interstate highway system is filled with cars, buses, and trucks. Much of the traffic passes through Illinois. We are at the *crossroads* of the interstate system. Can you think of why Illinois is a crossroads?

The Suburbs

Automobiles led to another new invention in the twentieth century—suburbs. Cars and highways let people look for houses farther away from the places they worked. They could drive to work, park their cars, and then drive home. The areas that grew up outside the cities, with rows and rows of houses, are called suburbs.

Television

Illinois factories began to build television sets. By 1960, almost every home in Illinois and the country had a TV. They watched programs such as *Howdy Doody*, *Milton Berle*, *Roy Rogers*, and sports events.

In 1958 Hula-Hoops went on sale for the first time. They were a big hit for boys and girls of the 50s.

Many suburbs that looked similar to this one grew up around Illinois cities.

Civil Rights

In the South, white people made laws that black people had to follow. The laws were called "Jim Crow" laws. Jim Crow laws were used to keep white people separate from black people. Black students had to attend schools just for blacks. Black people had to sit in the back of buses. Water fountains had signs above them that said "white only" or "black only." Movie theaters had "colored only" seats. Even many cemeteries were *segregated*.

Segregation took place in some northern states as well, but not by law. Blacks were not welcome in some Illinois suburbs. Real estate agents would not even show them certain houses. Banks would not give loans to black people. If black families did move into a home, garbage might be dumped on their lawns. People might break their windows.

As time went on, black leaders had enough. In Alabama, one such leader was Dr. Martin Luther King Jr. People invited King to speak in city after city. He helped them organize *protests*. He spoke about living the words found in the Declaration of Independence. He reminded the country that "all men are created equal." In Illinois, King spoke about equal housing and education for everyone. He led marches to call attention to these issues. The struggle for *civil rights* was picking up speed. It would continue throughout the rest of the century.

A Song of Freedom

We've been buked and we've been scorned,
We've been talked about, as sure as you're born.
But we'll never turn back, no,
We'll never turn back,
Until we've all been freed and
We have equality.

—Civil rights freedom song

Martin Luther King Jr. marches for civil rights. He is between the policeman and the other man at the front of the crowd.

Sadly, Dr. King was murdered in 1968. Some black people were so angry at the loss that they started riots on Chicago's South Side. Violence also broke out in Evanston, Maywood, Alton, Joliet, and Carbondale.

The Women's Movement

Women also fought for equal rights and opportunities during this time. Groups of women joined together to try to make women's wages equal to men's, elect more women to government offices, and give women other rights equal to men.

Some women, however, did not like the women's movement. They thought that more women going to work would not be good for children and families. They didn't think women should always be treated the same as men.

Ten thousand supporters held a rally in Springfield to try to pass the Equal Rights Amendment (ERA), which would give women equal rights under the law. But the amendment did not pass.

Women in many states spoke out for or against ERA. How do you think their actions made a difference? Do you think their actions made things easier for women today?

Ronald Reagan
1911–

Ronald Reagan was born in Tampico and spent most of his childhood in Dixon. His father was a shoe salesman. His mother taught him to read when he was very young. Reagan got a scholarship to a small college in Peoria. He studied economics.

He was student body president, captain of the swim team, and a football player. Then he became interested in acting and moved to California. After becoming a movie star, Reagan turned to politics. He was elected governor of California in 1966. Later he became the fortieth president of the United States.

He served two terms as president in the 1980s.

"We have every right to dream *heroic* dreams."
—Ronald Reagan

Other Wars

Since the end of World War II, people from Illinois have fought in the Korean War, the Vietnam War, and the Persian Gulf War.

The most unpopular war in U.S. history was the Vietnam War. People in Illinois and other states marched to protest the war in Vietnam. They believed our country was not fighting for a good reason.

After the Vietnam War, more than a million Vietnamese people left their country. They made a dangerous journey in small boats across the sea. Almost half of those who left Vietnam settled in the United States.

Recent Immigrants

Since the end of World War II, people have kept coming to Illinois to live. They have come from Mexico, Southeast Asia, the Pacific Islands, China, Japan, India, the Middle East, and many other countries. The story of a Southeast Asian immigrant might sound like this:

I am ten years old. My brother and I escaped from Cambodia. We had to run and hide in the jungle until we got to the ocean. Ten of our family started, but only four of us made it. When we got to the water, we had to pay hundreds of dollars to get on a small boat. We had little food and no belongings. We did not have enough money for all of us, so some had to stay behind. We hope to earn enough money to send for the others soon. It has been hard to get used to our new life here.

Some of Illinois' new immigrants come from countries in Southeast Asia.

The End of a Century

From the 1970s to the 90s Illinois continued to grow, and not just in the cities. In fact, big cities such as Chicago, Rockford, and Peoria lost people in the 70s and 80s. But the suburbs around Chicago and some areas in central and southern Illinois grew quickly.

Chicago experienced two important "firsts" in the 1980s. The people elected the first female mayor, Jane Byrne, and the first black mayor, Harold Washington. We will read more about these important people in the next chapter. Other important things were also happening in the world of Illinois *politics*. Ronald Reagan, the president of the United States in the 1980s, was from Illinois.

A Growing Hispanic Community

The 1990s brought a stream of immigrants from Mexico, South America, and Asia. By 1996 there were over one million Hispanic people living in Illinois. The main reason people came was to find better jobs. Many settled in farming regions, such as Brown, Johnson, and Williamson Counties. Others have chosen the suburbs of Chicago.

Luis Gutierrez is a U.S. Representative for a largely Hispanic district. He said of Illinois,

It is a state that has [been very open to] minorities, especially immigrants.

In 1993, the Upper Mississippi River flooded. Water flowed into many river towns and covered thousands of acres of farmland. It destroyed homes, businesses, crops, and natural ecosystems. After the flood, local and state officials met to discuss how to help the people recover from the damage.

A Rich Culture

Hispanics have brought their rich culture to our state. Here is an old Spanish folk song:

De colores,	Bright with colors,
de colores se listen los campos	bright with colors the mountains and valleys
en la primavera.	dress up in the springtime.
De colores,	Bright with colors,
de colores son los pajaritos que	bright with colors all the little birds
vienen de afuera.	fill the skies in the daytime.
De colores,	Bright with colors,
de colores es el arcoiris que vemos	bright with colors the rainbow brings joy
lucir.	with the glory of spring.

What are some examples of Hispanic culture in Illinois today?

Photo by John D. Ivanko

Bringing Words to Life

Writers take us to exciting places around the world and we don't even have to leave our seats. Illinois writers have educated, entertained, and touched people all around the world.

Carl Sandburg
1878–1967

Carl Sandburg was born in Galesburg after his parents came to America from Sweden. He was one of seven children. The family was so poor that Carl had to quit school when he was in the eighth grade. He delivered milk, laid bricks, harvested wheat, and shined shoes to help support his family.

Sandburg traveled up and down the Mississippi River gathering bits and pieces of songs. He put them together in what he called the "Rag Bag" of American songs. He also wrote many poems about Illinois and Chicago. He called Chicago the "City of the Big Shoulders" and "Hog Butcher for the World." He was impressed with how hard the people of Chicago worked. No job seemed impossible. Later, Sandburg was named poet *laureate* of Illinois, a very high honor.

Fog

The fog comes
on little cat feet.

It sits looking
over harbor and city
on silent ***haunches***
and then moves on.

Ernest Hemingway
1899–1961

Born in Oak Park, Hemingway is considered one of the most important writers in American literature. He wrote for newspapers and magazines. Later he wrote novels and short stories.

Hemingway often wrote about adventures he had in his own life. As a boy, his father taught him to hunt and fish the shores and forests surrounding Lake Michigan. He often wrote about hunting and fishing, as well as bull fights, war, safaris, and man's struggle against nature. Many of his stories are about courage.

In *The Old Man and the Sea*, an old fisherman works hard and long into the night to catch a very large, strong fish. Imagine looking up at the night sky from the middle of the sea and thinking these thoughts:

I am glad we do not have to try to kill the stars. Imagine if each day a man must try to kill the moon. The moon runs away. But imagine if a man each day should have to try to kill the sun? We are born lucky. Yes we are born lucky.

Hemingway graduated from Oak Park River Forest High School.

Gwendolyn Brooks
1917–

Though she was born in Kansas, Gwendolyn Brooks moved to Chicago when she was just a baby. She began to write poetry when she was only seven years old. In high school she had more than seventy-five poems published in *The Chicago Defender*. Brooks wrote about life on the South Side of Chicago. She was the first black woman to win the Pulitzer Prize. She became poet laureate of Illinois after Carl Sandburg.

Read the following lines from her poem "Corners on the Curving Sky," and then discuss with your classmates what it means to you.

Our earth is round, and, among other things
That means that you and I can hold
completely different
Points of view and both be right.

Other important Illinois writers include Edgar Lee Masters, Theodore Dreiser, John Dos Passos, Richard Wright, Edgar Rice Burroughs, and Saul Bellow.

Toward the Next Century

What will Illinois be like in the next century? The people of Illinois face many challenges in the years to come. Here are some things the people of Illinois are working on today:

- Cleaning up the environment so people can enjoy clean air and water.

- Protecting agricultural land so we can continue to raise crops.

- Providing better public housing.

- Taking care of children by improving schools and day care centers.

activity

Searching for the Answers—Your Own Interview

Interview someone who lived during World War II. You could choose a grandparent, family friend, neighbor, or church member.

Before the interview, get together with your class and make a list of questions you would like the person to answer. What kinds of things do you want to know? Here are some suggestions:

How old were you when the war started?

What do you remember most about the war?

How were things different after the war ended?

How might life be different today if the United States had not joined the war?

Questions for Review

1. Why did the United States enter World War II?

2. List three places in Illinois that made machines or equipment for the war.

3. What was the Holocaust?

4. Scientists did secret research on the atomic bomb at which Illinois university?

5. How did the automobile let people move to the suburbs?

6. What are civil rights? Give two examples of groups fighting for civil rights during this time period.

7. Who is Jane Byrne?

8. What two ethnic groups grew the most in Illinois in the 1990s?

Geography Tie-In

The United States went to war three times after World War II. On a separate sheet of paper, list the countries or regions against which the United States fought.

_____

_____

_____

Locate these three places on a map of the world.

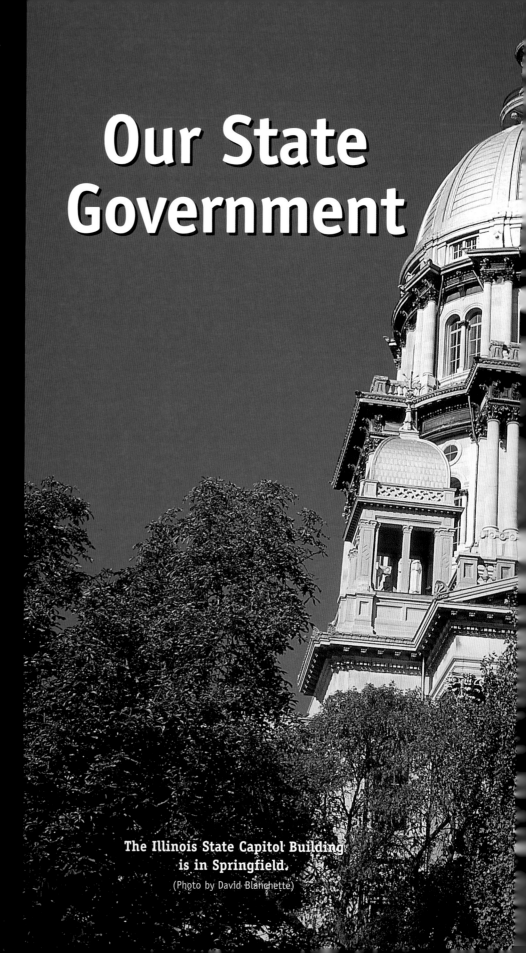

Our State Government

PEOPLE TO KNOW
Jesse Jackson Jr.
Carol Moseley-Braun
Governor Jim Edgar
Jane Byrne
Harold Washington
Richard M. Daley

PLACES TO LOCATE
Washington, D.C.
Arizona
Utah
California
Wisconsin
Louisiana
West Virginia
Springfield
Chicago
St. Charles

**The Illinois State Capitol Building
is in Springfield.**
(Photo by David Blanchette)

chapter 12

TERMS TO UNDERSTAND
representative democracy
representative
nominate
political
Independent
candidate
legislator
bill
majority
veto
militia
jury
population
local
ordinance
expense

Government for the Nation

Countries around the world have different kinds of governments. The kind that exists in the United States is only one kind. It makes sense to us. Other governments make sense to other people.

Over 200 years ago, when our country was deciding on its first government, Americans worried about having a government that was too powerful. They did not want a king, a queen, or a president to have all of the power. They wanted a way to rule themselves.

When a group of important men met to write the new Constitution, they gave the government of the United States of America only certain powers. Most of the power was given to the states. This way the people in one part of the country could make laws for themselves that might be different from the laws in another part of the country. The people thought this kind of government was best.

The writers of the Constitution did another very important thing. As part of the Constitution, they wrote a Bill of Rights. This listed rights that no government could take from them. Some of the rights were the right to belong to any religion they wanted to, to speak freely, and to write and print whatever they thought was important. These were rights that were not allowed in many other countries.

What do you think?

Why did the people think it was very important to add the Bill of Rights to their new Constitution?

Representatives of the People

How did the writers of the Constitution protect the people so one person could not have too much power? They decided to make the United States a *representative democracy*. This means that instead of all the people voting for the laws, the people could elect *representatives* to vote for them. This is like your class voting for a representative to go to a school student council meeting. The student council members from all of the classes then vote for certain things for the whole school.

In government, if the representatives don't vote the way the people want them to, the people will vote for someone else next time. This keeps the power in the hands of the people.

Who Can Vote?

Who can vote for representatives? Anyone can vote who is a citizen of the United States, is at least eighteen years old, and is registered (signed up to vote).

What do you think?

Do you think that eighteen-year-olds are responsible enough to vote for government leaders? Why or why not?

Jesse Jackson Jr. was voted to represent the Illinois people in the United States House of Representatives in Washington, D.C. in 1995. As a Democrat, Jackson worked on committees that studied banking, city problems, and small businesses. Before he became a congressman, Jackson started a program to encourage people of all political parties to vote.

What Are Political Parties?

To run for some government offices a person must first be *nominated* (named) by one of the *political* parties. Political parties are groups of people who have a lot of the same ideas about government. Most people choose either the Democratic Party or the Republican Party. Those are the two main parties in Illinois and in the rest of the United States.

There are also other parties, called third parties. As another choice, some citizens do not belong to any party. They run for office or vote as *Independents*. They don't often win elections, but they do get a chance to say what they think is important.

Once people have been chosen to run for office, they are called *candidates*. They raise money, make posters, buy TV and radio advertising, and give speeches. At voting time, the people vote for the candidates they think will do the best job.

Carol Moseley-Braun

Carol Moseley-Braun, a Democrat, was the first African American woman elected to the United States Senate in Washington, D.C. She grew up in Illinois. She said about her first day at school when she was a child:

"Everyone was bigger than me. When we went outside for recess, the other children wouldn't play with me because I couldn't catch the ball or run as fast. But I have an equally strong memory of my teacher, Miss Church. She took me inside and held me on her lap, and I felt much better. Years later, I was running for the Illinois House of Representatives and campaigning door-to-door —and guess who lived there? Miss Church!"

The elephant is the symbol for the Republican Party.   The donkey is the symbol for the Democratic Party.

Capital Cities

Springfield   Washington, D.C.

Government representatives meet and make laws in the capital city.

- The capital of the United States is Washington, D.C.
- The capital of Illinois is Springfield.

  People who live in Illinois have to follow the rules of both the United States and the Illinois governments.

Government for Illinois

The United States is made up of fifty states. Because they are in different places, they have different industries. They have different people with different ideas. Each state has different problems. Each state has its own state government.

In the West, for example, Arizona and Utah make laws about how water can be used. Water is very important there because they are desert states. California's government inspects crops for insects that might have been brought in with loads of fruits or vegetables. Wisconsin makes laws about fishing in its many lakes and rivers, and logging in its forests. Louisiana has laws about its docks, where ships load and unload their cargoes. West Virginia makes laws about safety in its coal mines. Illinois makes laws about its farms. All states decide how fast drivers can go on highways. They all decide how they will run their schools.

What do you think?

Representatives from Illinois and all of the fifty states go to Washington to make laws for the whole country. What problems might there be with so many people from so many places trying to make laws for everyone?

Our State Constitution

Illinois has a constitution that tells how our state government works. Our first constitution was written in 1818, when Illinois became a state. As Illinois grew and changed, new constitutions were written. Over the years, there have been four different constitutions for our state government. The last one was written and voted on by the people of Illinois in 1970.

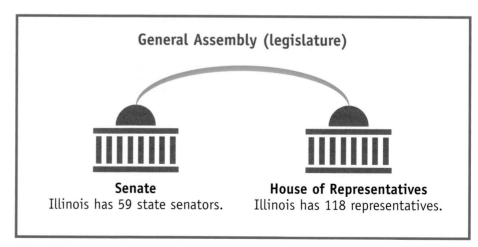

General Assembly (legislature)

Senate
Illinois has 59 state senators.

House of Representatives
Illinois has 118 representatives.

Branches of Government

One way the writers of the Constitution of the United States prevented a president from taking too much power was to divide the government into three parts, or branches. Our state government is also divided into three branches. Each branch has certain duties. This way the power is spread out.

Legislative Branch

The legislative branch makes the laws. The General Assembly meets each year to decide which **bills** become new laws. In Illinois the General Assembly is made of the Senate and the House of Representatives.

People from all over Illinois vote for their favorite representatives, or *legislators*. Then the people tell their representatives how they feel about problems by writing letters or e-mail, or by talking to them at their offices.

How a Bill Becomes a Law

A bill is a written idea for a new law. Someone writes the bill and takes it to either the Senate or the House. After legislators debate about the good and bad points of a bill, a vote is taken. If a *majority* votes "yes" on a bill, it goes to the other group. If a majority of that group also votes "'yes," it goes to the governor. If a majority of representatives votes "no" on the bill, it goes no further. It does not become law.

If the governor believes the bill would make a good law, he or she signs it and it becomes a new law for Illinois. If the governor does not believe the bill would make a good law, it is sent back to where it started. This is called a *veto*.

Senate

Bill

House of Representatives

Governor

Signs bill into law
or
vetos bill

Senate and House pass
by 3/5 majority

Senate

House of Representatives

Bill

Becomes law

After a veto, the legislators can vote again if they wish. If three of every five senators and representatives vote for the bill, it can become a law without going to the governor again. This is one way the power of making laws is shared by both branches of government. It is an important part of our constitution.

ILLINOIS PORTRAIT

Jim Edgar
1946–

Growing up in Charleston, Jim Edgar served as governor from 1991 to 1998. One of his goals was to help children. While he was governor, the state gave more tax money to schools and started charter schools. Edgar and his wife Brenda led efforts to change adoption laws so more children without families could become permanent members of good homes. Under his leadership, more than 100,000 families moved from welfare rolls to jobs. Edgar also worked for Conservation 2000, a program to protect Illinois land and water. The state protected thousands of acres of land to use as wildlife habitats and developed other land as outdoor recreation areas for people. A very popular governor, Edgar was re-elected in a record-breaking victory.

Executive Branch

The executive branch carries out the laws. The governor is the head of the executive branch and is elected by the people of Illinois. Here is a list of some jobs the governor does. Which do you think are most important?

- Sees that state laws are carried out.
- Suggests bills to the General Assembly.
- Gives a state budget (tells how money will be spent) to the General Assembly.
- Signs bills into law or vetoes (rejects) them.
- Calls the General Assembly into special extra sessions.
- Is the chief of the state *militia* (army).
- Can grant a pardon (forgiveness) to people found guilty of a crime. It may keep them out of jail!
- Leads his or her own political party.

Many people help the governor in the executive branch. Some are needed to collect tax money. Others help people get licenses to drive automobiles and run businesses. Workers in the executive branch help farmers market their products. They inspect farm animals to be sure they are healthy. Others work for our state parks and roads. There are people who work in welfare, health, and education. When the Mississippi River overflowed in 1993, the state militia was called by the governor to help people move to a safe place.

Judicial Branch

The courts make up the judicial branch of our state's government. The judicial branch interprets the laws. The judges who are in charge of the courts are elected by the people of Illinois.

Courts decide if a person is guilty of a crime. The judge and often a *jury* listen to the reports of police officers. They listen to other people who might have been involved. After everyone has been heard, the jury must decide if the person on trial is guilty or not. If the person is found guilty of the crime, the judge decides how the person should be punished.

In another kind of case, a person might feel that he or she has not been treated fairly. A person might ask the courts to decide who was to blame for an accident. The court will listen to both sides and then decide on a way to settle the argument.

activity

You Be the Judge!

A judge is a very important person. He or she must listen carefully to both sides before deciding what to do. The judge can fine people, send people to jail, or just talk to them about being good citizens. In each case, a judge uses the laws that were written by the legislators to help decide what to do.

Now it is your turn to be the judge. Read the story. Then write how you would have the boys settle their problem.

Jason rides his shiny new black and silver bike to school. He carefully locks it up. After school, his friend Matthew asks to borrow the bike for a while. Jason agrees and tells Matthew to take good care of it and to bring it back before dark.

Matthew enjoys riding the bike and stays out late. When he gets home it is about dark and his family is calling him in for the night. Matthew lays the bike down on the ground and goes in. In the morning, the bike is gone. It has been stolen.

Jason is very upset about his new bike. He thinks Matthew and his family should buy him a new one. Matthew says his family doesn't have enough money to buy a new bike. He says it was too dark to return the bike the night before. He says he had planned to go back outside later and put the bike in a safe place, but he forgot. He says it was not his fault the bike was stolen.

Levels of Government

In some places, wheat and corn fields cover the land. In other places, skyscrapers and apartment buildings are all you can see. Cities might have a very high *population*, with roads and sidewalks crowded with cars and people. Other places are quiet, with very few people.

Because different places have different needs, *local* governments are important. Local governments are governments close to home. County and city governments are both local governments because they are closer to home than the state government in Springfield. They are also closer to home than the U.S. government in Washington, D.C.

In the United States there are several levels of government—national, state, and local. Each level has the three branches of government (executive, legislative, judicial).

Chicago's first female mayor was Jane Byrne. A mayor is part of which **level** of government? A mayor is part of which **branch** of government?

LEVEL	HEAD OF THE EXECUTIVE BRANCH
United States	President
State	Governor
City	Mayor

ILLINOIS PORTRAIT

Harold Washington
1922–1987

Chicago's mayor from 1983–1987 went to DuSable High School. Raised mostly by his father and his stepmother, Washington was smart, witty, and friendly. He was the only black student in his class at Northwestern University Law School. Washington worked hard, and was later voted in as an Illinois representative and then a senator. He ran for mayor of Chicago, but lost that election. Washington ran again for mayor of Chicago. This time he won. He became Chicago's first black mayor. He worked to reduce crime, help public education, and develop better neighborhoods. After winning the same office again in the next election, Washington died suddenly of a heart attack.

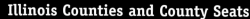

Illinois Counties and County Seats

Look at the map and find your county and your county seat. Have you ever visited the courthouse there? What are the counties that border your county? See if you can find out where your county got its name.

County Government

Illinois is divided into 102 counties. Each county has a town that is the county seat. There is usually a courthouse there, where the courts are located. Births, deaths, and marriages are recorded at the courthouse. If your family owns property, a map of your property is recorded in your county courthouse.

City Government

Another kind of local government even closer to home is city government. There are different kinds of city governments. Cities are usually run by a mayor or a city manager, with a city council. Larger cities have larger governments than small towns. Cities make rules about what kinds of buildings can be built in different regions of the city. They often keep houses separate from businesses. They make sure schools are in safe places. They make laws about speed limits in the city.

St. Charles—Local Government in Action

The Municipal Building in St. Charles is along the Fox River.

Pioneers started St. Charles on the Fox River. They picked a place where Potawatomi, Sauk, and Fox Indians had crossed the river on their way to and from Lake Michigan. In 1850 the tiny pioneer settlement became a village. In 1874 the people held a special vote and it became a city. At that time, St. Charles picked its first mayor and city council.

Life was different in 1874 than it is today. Animals played an important part in the lives of almost everyone. People around St. Charles were dairy farmers. They kept cows for milking. They used horses for transportation and farm work. The city council had to make rules about animals. When farm animals began roaming through the city, a law was passed by the city council. It said the cows, pigs, sheep, and horses had to be fenced in. Another *ordinance* said that no one could roll a hoop or fly a kite where horses might get scared.

Over the years, local government has become a larger part of people's lives in St. Charles. A school district was set up so children would have good schools to attend. A park district was created so people could have beautiful parks and fun things to do. A modern fire department was created to protect the people and buildings of the city. If you walk through St. Charles today, you will see how local government works.

ILLINOIS PORTRAIT

Richard M. Daley
1942–

Chicago's mayor Richard M. Daley grew up in a family of seven children. His father was also mayor of Chicago. In 1972 he was elected to the Illinois Senate, where he led the fight to remove the sales tax on food and medicine. In 1989 he was elected as mayor of Chicago and was re-elected in 1991 and 1995. Daley made a goal of making schools better and safer. He assigned police officers to schools. To help the city he added 1,600 more police officers to help stop crime. Starting anti-gang programs, eliminating graffiti, and tearing down old buildings to use the space for parks were part of his plan. Money from a cigarette tax went to provide more beds for the homeless. Helping his city has won Mayor Daley many national awards.

What do you think?

Can you think of city laws, sometimes called ordinances, that affect you? They might have to do with speed limits, crosswalks, bike licenses, dog licenses, garbage pick-up, busses or taxis, or rules for your park or swimming pool. Why do you think these laws were passed? Which laws do you agree with? Which ones would you like to change, and why?

Taxes Pay for Services

The Illinois state constitution gives the state, county, and city governments the power to collect taxes. Tax money pays for the services local governments provide.

Taxes come in many forms. People and businesses pay taxes on their income. Those who have large incomes are expected to pay more income tax than those who have smaller incomes. When you buy new clothes or toys at stores or eat at restaurants, you pay a sales tax. Our license plate fees and highway tolls also are a kind of tax. Each county collects taxes on land, homes, apartment buildings, office buildings, and stores. These are called property taxes.

What is tax money used for? Taxes pay for building local streets and plowing snow. Taxes pay for libraries where you can check out books. They pay for parks where you can play ball and have picnics. Taxes even pay for the fireworks you see on the Fourth of July.

Cities arrange for a clean water supply for people to use. They arrange to have your garbage picked up. Cities usually get involved in recreation, too. If you play soccer or basketball on a city team, you are using a city service. If you swim in a city pool, you are using your local government services.

One of the most important things taxes pay for is education. If you go to a public school, your school building, your books, and even your teacher are paid for with tax money. If you go to a private school, your parents have to pay for these things.

Living within a Budget

Do your parents give you an allowance? Do you ever earn money? What do you use it for? If you have to pay for certain things with your own money, you know the importance of living within your budget. A budget is a plan for using your money in the best way possible. Budgets show how much money you will receive and how you plan to use that money.

Financing the State

Where the money comes from:

income tax

property tax

sales tax

gas tax

license fees

Where the money goes:

government employees

schools

highways

farm programs

health care

postal service

unemployment

public welfare

schools

road work

libraries

parks

police and fire protection

Governments must also prepare budgets. State, county, and city governments must each plan for all the money they will receive. This is called their income. Then they plan how they will spend the money. This is very difficult because different people want different things. Some people, for instance, want more free health clinics. Some want more money for school supplies such as books and computers. Some people want the roads to be repaired more often. Some want more welfare money for families with children. Other people think there is already too much money spent on welfare. There is never enough money to take care of everything people want from the government.

What happens when you have no money left from your allowance and still want to buy something? Do you ever borrow money from your parents? How do you pay them back? Sometimes, governments also need to borrow money. They make a budget and then they learn that their *expenses* are larger than their incomes. When this happens, they might borrow money.

A government might buy less so that they do not have to borrow money. Schools sometimes buy fewer library books because they cannot afford the books they wanted. They might put off hiring more teachers for the same reason.

Living within a budget forces us to make tough choices. Budgets help us plan ahead so we buy the things we really need the most.

activity

Get Involved!

Illinois is only as good as its people. That means all of the people—male and female, people of all races, rich and poor, young and old—must be good citizens. They need to get involved in government and help others whenever they can.

What can you do? Discuss these ideas as a class and make a list on the board. Can you think of other things?

- Obey all of your family and school rules.

- Obey the law all of the time.

- Always tell the truth.

- Be polite and helpful to everyone.

- Never litter.

- Help keep your own home and yard clean.

- Never make graffiti (writing on walls or buildings).

- Never ruin property.

- Tell adults in your family to vote.

- Tell your representatives what you want them to do (by letter or e-mail).

- Write a letter to the editor of a newspaper. Letters from kids often get published!

- Talk with adults about what is going on in government, especially in your town.

activity

Word Power!
Do you understand all of the vocabulary words in this chapter? On a separate piece of paper, write the words on the list below. Before each word, write the letter of its correct meaning. If you need help, use the glossary at the end of this book.

1. candidate
2. courthouse
3. jury
4. legislator
5. local
6. nominate
7. ordinance
8. political
9. representative
10. veto

a. A person elected to make laws
b. A building where judges and juries meet
c. A person who seeks an office
d. Near home
e. Citizens who decide a case in a courtroom
f. To choose someone to run as a candidate
g. To reject a bill
h. A city rule or law
i. Having to do with government
j. A person elected to vote for other people

Questions for Review

1. What do representatives do?

2. In order to vote, you must be how old?

3. What are the two largest political parties in the U.S. today?

4. What branch of government makes laws for Illinois?

5. A law starts out as a _____ .

6. Who (what office) is head of the executive branch of the country? A state? A city?

7. What can a governor do if he or she does not want a bill to become a law?

8. Courts are part of which branch?

9. List two examples of local government.

10. Services such as police and schools are paid for with _____ money.

Geography Tie-In

On a wall map in your classroom, locate Springfield, our state capital, and Washington, D.C., our nation's capital. How far do our representatives have to travel to get to Washington? What method of travel do they probably use? Why?

THE TIME
1840–2000

PEOPLE TO KNOW
George E. Johnson
Oprah Winfrey
Ray Kroc
Anton Finkl
Edward O'Hare
Wallace D. Abbott

PLACES TO LOCATE
Des Plaines
Lake Michigan
Mississippi River
Chicago River
Des Plaines River
Illinois & Michigan Canal
Sanitary and Ship Canal
Illinois Waterway
St. Lawrence Seaway
Glenview
Northbrook
Oak Brook
Peoria
Rockford
Decatur
Chicago

Making a Living in Illinois

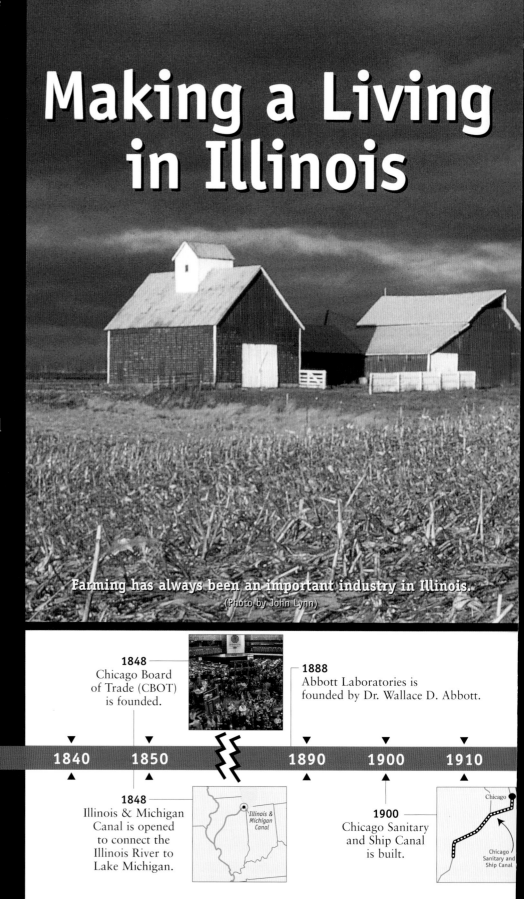

Farming has always been an important industry in Illinois.
(Photo by John Lynn)

timeline of events

1848
Chicago Board of Trade (CBOT) is founded.

1888
Abbott Laboratories is founded by Dr. Wallace D. Abbott.

1840   1850   1890   1900   1910

1848
Illinois & Michigan Canal is opened to connect the Illinois River to Lake Michigan.

Illinois & Michigan Canal

1900
Chicago Sanitary and Ship Canal is built.

Chicago

Chicago Sanitary and Ship Canal

chapter 13

TERMS TO UNDERSTAND
goods
product
service
capitalism
free enterprise
employee
wage
salary
profit
entrepreneur
philanthropy
forge
mortar
grid
global

1949
Orchard Place is renamed Chicago O'Hare
International Airport.

1963
New airport facility at
O'Hare is dedicated.

1985
*The
Oprah
Winfrey
Show*
begins.

1920   1930   1940   1950   1960   1970   1980   1990   2000

1933
Illinois Waterway
is completed,
connecting the Great
Lakes with the
Mississippi River.

1954 Johnson Products is founded in Chicago.

1955 First McDonald's restaurant opens in Des Plaines.

1959 St. Lawrence Seaway is opened, connecting
the Great Lakes to the Atlantic Ocean.

Economics for Everyone

People have needs. They also have wants. They need food, clothing, and shelter. They want things like cars, books, toys, and bicycles. These are called **goods**, or **products**. People also need medical care from doctors and nurses. They need education from teachers. They may want help repairing their washing machine or fixing a broken window. These are called **services**. Economics is the study of how people get the goods and services that they need and want.

An economic system is a way of producing and selling the goods and services people need and want. There are many different economic systems. Different countries in the world use different systems. The United States has what is called a **capitalistic** or **free enterprise** system. Here is how it works:

People in the United States own the factories and companies that produce goods and services. The business is the property of the owner. Owners decide what to produce and how much to charge for it. They decide where to do business. They decide who they want to help them. They are in charge of selling the product, too.

Business owners usually hire other people, called **employees**, to work for them. The owner pays the employees a **wage**, or a **salary**. Most adults in the United States are employees.

Making a Profit

How do business owners make money? Usually they sell what their employees produce. They can sell goods or a service. The electric company sells electricity. Dentists sell their services to fix your teeth.

The money earned after expenses are subtracted is called a **profit**. People who make shoes have to pay for the leather, the glue, the machines, and the building. These are expenses. They have to pay themselves for all the work involved in making the shoes. They must sell the shoes for more than it costs to make them. If not, they will have a loss instead of a profit. They will soon be out of business.

Workers expect the company to pay them fairly. They expect medical insurance and vacation pay. They want the company to provide a clean safe place to work.

Owners also expect things from their employees. They want their workers to come on time, work hard, and do good work. They want them to be trained for the job. They don't want workers to steal supplies from them or waste time.

Making and selling shoes was one way of earning a profit. What clues show that this photo was taken a long time ago?

Supply and Demand

How do business owners decide how much to charge for their products? The selling price depends on a lot of things. The price has to be more than what it cost the company to make the item so the business will make a profit. Sometimes the price also depends on how much of something there is. If a toy becomes so popular that a company cannot make enough for everyone who wants it, the company can sell the toy for a higher price. People will be willing to pay more to get it. This is called the rule of supply and demand.

Sometimes a company has to lower its prices. Maybe a company makes bicycles but people don't buy very many of them. So the company has a lot of extra bicycles sitting around. They might lower the price to get people to buy them. Or maybe there are two companies that make bicycles. One of the companies might lower its price to get people to buy from it instead of from the other company.

Sometimes there is only one company that produces a certain product. Then the owners can charge about whatever price they want. If buyers want that product or service, they will have to pay whatever price the company charges.

When there is a lot of something, the cost can be lower. If there is not very much of something, the cost is usually higher.

Methods Used in Advertising

Color and excitement
The ad is bright and colorful so people will notice it. The product seems fun and exciting.

Repetition
The ad says a name or slogan over and over.

Social appeal
The ad suggests that if you use a certain product you will look nice and have a lot of friends.

Humor
People like and remember things that are funny.

Music
People remember short tunes.

Consumers Buy Products and Services

People are workers. They are also consumers. A consumer is a person who buys things. Anyone who spends money is a consumer. Are you a consumer? What kinds of things do you buy with your money?

Most people want to spend their money wisely. They compare different brands to get the best for their money. They also compare prices at different stores.

Stores try to get consumers to shop in their stores by advertising. Advertising may be on the radio, on TV, or on billboards beside the highways and on the sides of buildings. You see and hear it everywhere. Being a wise consumer means understanding how advertising works. Have you ever bought something because the advertisement made it seem exciting? And then you found out it wasn't? It seemed like the commercial lied. Do you believe everything a commercial says? What does the ad below try to get you to believe about wearing *Wild Things* Sunglasses?

The sunglasses are patterned after the colorful markings of our jungle friends: the tiger, cheetah, zebra, jaguar, and boa. These glasses also block out harmful UV rays. A percentage of the profits goes to support zoos. Get your *Wild Things* today and help our fellow creatures have a future. (Not available on any other planet.)

Economics in Early Illinois

Today, Illinois businesses use the free enterprise system, like everywhere else in the United States. However, a system of free enterprise did not always exist here.

American Indians did not believe in private ownership. They said that no one had the right to own land and keep it for himself. The land and everything on it was to be shared by everyone. No one was to have more of anything than anyone else.

When fur traders came to Illinois, they started taking land and resources for themselves. They used the beavers in the area to make their own personal fortunes. Even though they did not own the land or beavers, they took it for themselves.

Early settlers started buying and selling goods such as flour, corn, and household items. Stores opened up in towns all across Illinois. Soon Illinois' economic system was much like that in other places in the U.S.

People made money by working for someone else, or by opening their own businesses. This is a butcher shop in 1909. What things in the picture are different from what you see in a store today?

Immigrants Become Entrepreneurs

When immigrants came to this country, most of them got jobs working for other people. The pay was usually very low. If they did not know the language, the men and women had to do jobs that no one else wanted. People who were doctors, university professors, or skilled furniture makers in the old country ended up cleaning floors, laying railroad track, or working in mines in America. It was a hard way to live.

People wanted better work. Thousands of immigrants became *entrepreneurs*. An entrepreneur is someone who has an idea and the courage to start a business. Entrepreneurs work for themselves. Usually the whole family helped with the business. Even the children sewed, hammered, chopped, ran errands, or whatever needed to be done. When the business grew, the family hired other employees.

Many immigrants began their businesses with a skill they had learned in their old country. Perhaps an Italian baker opened his own bakery here. Perhaps a tailor from Greece opened her own clothing store. People who made furniture in Germany could make furniture here and sell it themselves. If a group of furniture makers started a business together they could make more tables, chairs, and cupboards. Together they could have a good business.

Some entrepreneurs sold goods. Maybe they made hats, rugs, or wagons. Maybe they farmed and sold the extra wheat or apples.

Some entrepreneurs sold services. They may have delivered groceries, painted homes, or taught classes. They may have opened their own barbershops and cut hair.

Immigrants often used the skills they already knew before they came here. This man from Germany is making furniture to sell.

Illinois Entrepreneurs

Illinois is the home of many businesses, industries, and entrepreneurs. There are banks, food processing plants, and farm machinery factories. John Deere and Marshall Field are famous entrepreneurs. They both left their mark on Illinois. Other entrepreneurs have also done important things. Here are a few of them.

GEORGE E. JOHNSON

In 1954, George Johnson borrowed $250 to found Johnson Products, a company that makes hair care products for African Americans. Johnson's workers did many experiments to develop special hair care products. The company has developed 200 products, including Gentle Treatment, Ultra Sheen, and Ultra Star.

In 1971, Johnson Products became the only African American advertiser to sponsor a television show—*Soul Train*. Johnson Products is headquartered on Chicago's South Side.

OPRAH WINFREY

Oprah Winfrey became the first African American woman to anchor the local news in Nashville, Tennessee. In 1984 she became the host of the talk show, *A.M. Chicago*. In 1985, she developed her own talk show called *The Oprah Winfrey Show*. Her show has become the highest-rated talk show in television history.

Winfrey is active in **philanthropy**, encourages people to volunteer to help others, supports education, and raises money for scholarships. She says she wants her television program and the money it makes to make a difference in people's lives.

Factors of Production

There are four things that must come together before something is sold as a good or service. These things are called factors of production. Factors of production are land, labor, capital goods, and entrepreneurship. Let's learn what these things mean:

Land (natural resources)
People use the term "land" to mean anything that is found in nature. If you are making chairs, you might use wood. It is from the land. If you are making teddy bears and need cotton to stuff them, you use cotton. Cotton and wood are both natural resources that grow on the land.

Labor
To provide goods and services, there must be labor. Labor is the work that people do. Even if you bought a robot, it took labor to make it. Someone built it and someone sold it. Carpenters, teachers, sales people, lawyers, secretaries, actors, race car drivers, and basketball players all do labor.

Capital Goods
When you use something that is already made to make something else, you are using a capital good. The hammer and nails a carpenter uses are capital goods. The paint, canvas, and brushes an artist uses are capital goods. The money needed to run a business is also called capital.

Entrepreneurship
Entrepreneurship is owning and running a business. It often starts with an idea. The person must be willing to take a risk to make the idea work. Entrepreneurs use land, labor, and capital goods to make money.

RAY KROC

Ray Kroc started a company that almost everyone around the world would recognize— McDonald's Corporation. Kroc started out working for a company that sold a new milk shake machine called the "multimixer." The mixers were becoming popular at restaurants. Kroc visited a hamburger shop that sold milk shakes, along with burgers and french fries. The shop was owned by a pair of brothers named Mac and Dick McDonald. Ray Kroc convinced the brothers to let him start a chain of drive in restaurants just like theirs.

Kroc opened his first restaurant in Des Plaines in 1955. The restaurant made $366.12 that first day. Today, the Des Plaines restaurant is a museum with McDonald's items, including the multimixer.

Ray Kroc was a great businessman who did more than sell Big Macs. He donated lots of money to charities and started the Ronald McDonald House. Families of sick children can stay there while their children are in the hospital.

ANTON FINKL

German immigrant Anton Finkl started a company in Illinois called A. Finkl & Sons Co. His company has become one of the largest custom *forges* in the United States. This means that it specializes in making and processing steel.

Finkl arrived in Chicago in 1871, the same year as the Great Fire. He found work as a brick cleaner, using a chisel he invented to clean *mortar* off bricks. After Chicago's rubble was cleared, he started his own blacksmithing business. Through the years, A. Finkl & Sons Co. has grown. The company now uses modern technology to work with steel.

Finkl's company does more than make steel. The people who work there recycle waste materials and participate in a project to plant trees in Illinois and Wisconsin.

activity

Factors of Production and Corn

You know that Illinois farmers provide corn. They plow the fields, plant the corn, weed, and water the crops as they grow. At harvest time, farmers use farm machinery to pick the corn. Trucks then take the corn to the markets and food processing plants. Then the corn products are shipped to Illinois cities, other states, and other countries. The corn products may end up on your table as corn oil, corn on the cob, or even popcorn.

It is hard work to produce corn. What factors of production were needed by the corn industry?

Many factors must come together for an Illinois harvest.

Transportation Hub of the Nation

Transportation of natural resources and products is very important for business. Without good transportation, business would almost stop. Illinois is a major hub of transportation for the United States. Illinois has interstate highways, an important railroad system, and the busiest airport in the world. Lake Michigan and the Mississippi River are major transportation routes. This makes it easy for people to get around the state of Illinois. This makes it easy to get from Illinois to anywhere in the world.

When President John F. Kennedy dedicated a new facility at O'Hare in 1963, he said, **"This is an extraordinary airport, extraordinary city, and an extraordinary country, and it [O'Hare] could be classed as one of the wonders of the modern world."**

Look at a road map of the United States. Which two states are difficult or impossible to drive to from Illinois?

O'Hare—The Busiest Airport in the World

In 1949 an airstrip that wasn't used much had its name changed from Orchard Place to Chicago O'Hare International Airport. It was named for Lieutenant Commander O'Hare, a United States Navy pilot. He was awarded the Congressional Medal of Honor for his heroic actions during World War II.

O'Hare has grown into the nation's busiest airport. But even though O'Hare has outgrown its roots, it still has a link to the past. O'Hare's airport code used on tickets and baggage tags is still ORD, for the old Orchard Place airport.

Growth of a Railroad—Growth of a State

When the railroad came to Illinois, thousands of settlers were attracted to the land along the railroad. Towns like Centralia, Champaign, Carbondale, and Matoon grew around railroad junctions. Chicago became the hub of this new and vast railroad system. The state grew and prospered.

Today railroads carry agricultural products, raw materials, and manufactured goods to the nation. Of course, they also transport people.

On the Road

Illinois has a large network of highways and roads. We have many miles of toll roads, too. These are highways that you pay a fee to use.

The city of Chicago alone has about 4,000 miles of streets. These streets are set up in a *grid* pattern. A grid is a framework of crisscrossed lines or bars. The houses and buildings are numbered so that it is very easy to find your way around the streets of Chicago.

Illinois is not only the hub of the nation's railroads, it also lies at the heart of the nation's interstate highway system. Three highways that run from coast to coast pass right through Illinois. These highways are joined by many major interstate highways that run north to south.

Our highway system makes Illinois a great place for trucking lines. Trucks, like trains, are a reliable and inexpensive way to transport goods. Thousands of trucking lines operate in Illinois. They help keep our economy strong.

Illinois Waterways

Rivers Link Us to the World

Illinois waterways make it possible for the Atlantic Ocean to be linked to the Mississippi River, but it wasn't always that way. Canals had to be built to link the waters together.

Illinois is located right between the Great Lakes and the Mississippi River. In 1848, the Illinois & Michigan Canal was opened to connect the Illinois River to Lake Michigan. This link makes it possible to ship goods that are grown or manufactured in Illinois to places all over the country and the world.

In 1900 the Sanitary and Ship Canal was built. This helped solve the problem of water pollution in Lake Michigan. It also connected Lake Michigan to the Des Plaines River.

In 1933 the Illinois Waterway was completed. The Illinois Waterway is part of a larger system of waterways and canals. They make it possible to ship goods from Canada all the way to the Gulf of Mexico and then to the Atlantic Ocean. It was very important to have this all-water route since it was often faster and cheaper to transport goods over water than over land.

St. Lawrence Seaway

In 1959 the St. Lawrence Seaway was opened. It was built to connect the Atlantic Ocean to the Great Lakes by water. The St. Lawrence Seaway, along with the Illinois Waterway, allows ships coming from the Atlantic Ocean to reach cities such as Toronto, Cleveland, Detroit, Milwaukee, Duluth, and, of course, Chicago. This seaway makes it possible to move goods between the heartland of America and international markets overseas. Iron ore, coal, grain, machinery, electronic equipment, and transportation equipment are just some of the products that the Midwest exports.

These barges use Illinois waterways to transport freight to and from Illinois.

Photo by John Lynn

Illinois Companies

Chicago is a major center of industry. Major companies are headquartered in many other Illinois cities as well. Here are just a few of them.

CITY	COMPANY
Glenview	Kraft Inc.
Northbrook	Allstate Insurance
Oak Brook	Sunbeam Corporation
Peoria	Caterpillar Inc.
Rockford	Sunstrand Corporation
Decatur	Archer Daniels Midland Company

Making a Living Today

When Illinois first became a state, almost everyone farmed. Farming is still very important here. But today, most people work in either manufacturing or service jobs. As cities have become more important, the agricultural lifestyle has slowly been replaced by the business world of the city. Illinois, and Chicago especially, has been a leader in this shift.

What do you think?

• Do you think there should be a return to the agricultural lifestyle that existed when our state was young?

• What advantages or disadvantages might there be to a more rural (farm) lifestyle?

Manufacturing

Food processing is one of the major manufacturing industries in Illinois. One Illinois company, Archer Daniels Midland (ADM), is a *global* food processor. They produce enough food ingredients to feed 130 million people a day. ADM's products include vegetable oil, corn oil, soy products used in baby formula, high fructose corn syrup used in soft drinks and other sweets, wheat flour, and animal feed.

Another modern industry that has its roots in Illinois is Abbott Laboratories. Founded by Dr. Wallace D. Abbott in Chicago in 1888, this company is a major producer of different drugs and medicines. This was one of the first companies to distribute penicillin. Other products include Ensure liquid food products and Similac baby formula.

From the Farm to Your Table

Not only is Illinois a leader in agriculture, but it is also a leader in processing farm goods into food products we use every day. You can enjoy a whole day of meals brought to you by the food companies of Illinois.

Breakfast: oatmeal from Quaker Oats.

Lunch: a peanut butter sandwich made with Peter Pan peanut butter from Swift-Eckrich and bread from Pepperidge Farms.

Dinner: macaroni and cheese dinner from Kraft with hot dogs from Oscar Meyer.

Midnight snack: cookies from Keebler and milk from Deans.

Enjoy Illinois!

When people visit Illinois from other states and countries, they may eat at a restaurant in Peoria, visit the Cahokia Mounds, visit Lincoln's home in Springfield, or go to the Sears Tower and a Bulls basketball game in Chicago. These are all part of a major industry: tourism.

Tourism provides jobs. Tourism also brings money into the state. Tourists spend money on transportation, lodging, food, entertainment, and recreation.

▶ Photo by John Lynn

Tourism adds money to Illinois' economy.

Chicago Board of Trade

▶ Photo by John D. Ivanko

The price you pay for goods depends on how the value of a product is determined. The Chicago Board of Trade is a major center of buying and selling products such as wheat, soybeans, and corn. At the Chicago Board of Trade, these products are called futures. Futures are promises to buy or sell at a set price in the future. The price of these futures determines how much you, the consumer, will pay for a product.

This is how it works: Let's say a farmer is growing corn. Many factors will affect the supply and demand for the corn, which causes the price to rise and fall. These factors include new products, weather, and the products of other farmers. The farmer will watch the prices of corn at the Chicago Board of Trade and when he sees a price he likes, he agrees to deliver his corn at that price in the future.

The floor of the Chicago Board of Trade is an exciting place.

The Illinois Adventure!

This book is a good example of how free enterprise economics works. Illinois' students needed a new Illinois history book. A company decided to produce the book. The owner of the company hired people to work on the book. Everyone wanted it to be a book children would really like. They worked hard to make it interesting and tell the true story of Illinois. They also hoped the teachers would like the book enough to buy it, so the company would make a profit.

It took the services and products of many people in different parts of the world to make the book. Here is what happened.

The authors in Illinois and North Carolina studied about Illinois' history. They went to libraries and read books about Illinois. They read the diaries of people who had lived here a long time ago. The authors typed the words on computers. The editor in Massachusetts was in charge of making sure the spelling and punctuation were right. She found the photographs. She hired an artist to draw some of the pictures. A different artist, who lives in Minnesota, used a computer to arrange the words and pictures on each page. She chose photos to put on the cover. All of these things took over a year to do.

When the book was ready to be printed, it was sent across the Pacific Ocean to Hong Kong. The paper came from trees in Asia. Someone made and sold the ink to the printer. Many workers there printed the book on huge presses. They used machines to sew the pages together and glue the covers on. After about four months the books were brought to America on a ship. The ship landed in San Francisco. Then large boxes of books were brought to Illinois in trucks.

All of the people who worked on the book had to be paid for their services. All of the machines, computers, paper, and even ink had to be paid for. Where did the money come from?

You and your friends are the consumers. Your school paid for your books. The school got the money from the government. The government got the money from taxes. The taxes were paid by the adults in your town. The people earned the money to pay their taxes from their jobs or businesses.

So there you have it. People work hard to provide the goods and services other people need. The work makes them feel good about themselves. It provides money for the workers' families. The work helps provide for the needs of everyone.

activity

Goods and Services

Goods are things that are made in factories, workshops, or even at home. They are then sold for money. Shoes, pencils, televisions, and dog collars are all goods. People make money by making and selling goods.

Services are things that people do for other people. Dentists, sales clerks, umpires, coaches, and your teachers provide services. People earn money by providing services.

Don't be fooled! Many people who provide a service also use goods. The sales clerk, for example, is providing a service by selling shoes. The shoes are goods, but the sales clerk provides a service by selling them to you.

On a separate piece of paper, number from one to fourteen. Write 'G' for goods or 'S' for services for each job listed below.

1. Works with plumbing
2. Collects the garbage
3. Teaches students
4. Manufactures paint
5. Paints pictures to sell
6. Makes engines for cars
7. Repairs cars
8. Wraps cheese in a factory
9. Delivers cheese to grocery stores
10. Makes telephones
11. Repairs telephones
12. Manufactures light bulbs
13. Sells light bulbs
14. What you would like to do when you grow up

Questions for Review

1. What is the difference between a good and a service?

2. Briefly explain how a capitalistic, free enterprise system works.

3. Name three methods used in advertising to attract consumers.

4. List the four factors of production. Give an example of each.

5. Briefly describe one Illinois entrepreneur, either from the chapter or of your own choosing.

6. What is the airport code for O'Hare? Why?

7. What bodies of water did the St. Lawrence Seaway connect?

8. Name one major industry in Illinois. Name one company involved in that industry.

Geography Tie-In

1. What geographical factors make one area better for farming and another area better for manufacturing?

2. How does the location of Illinois make it a center for trade and transportation?

GLOSSARY

abolish: to put an end to

abolitionist: a person against slavery

adapt: to change to fit new ways

advancement: improvement; promotion

alliance: an agreement between two or more groups of people to unite for a specific purpose

ally: a nation or group united with another nation or group for a common cause

ambitious: showing an eager desire for success, honor, or power

animated: designed as a cartoon

archaeologist: a scientist who learns about ancient people by studying the things they left behind

architect: a person who designs buildings

artifact: an object made by people long ago

atomic: relating to nuclear energy and atomic bombs

barracks: a building or group of buildings for lodging soldiers

barter: to exchange one thing for another without the use of money

bill: a written idea for a law

brawny: muscular and strong

canal: a waterway made by people rather than nature

candidate: a person who seeks an office

capitalism: a system in which people, not the government, own the land and wealth and businesses compete with each other to make a profit

cargo: goods that are being transported

charity: an institution for helping the needy

Christianity: the religion of Christians; believing in Jesus Christ

civil rights: the rights that citizens are entitled to

civilian: a citizen who isn't in the army

clan: a group of people united by a common interest or relationship

colony: a territory under the control of another nation

combat: a fight between individuals or groups

community: a group of people living together

conflict: a disagreement or struggle

conserve: to keep in good condition

constitution: the written rights and laws of a group

consumer: a person who buys and uses things

continent: one of the seven large land areas of the world

convert: to change another person's beliefs

credit: trust given to a customer for future payment

crossroads: the place where roads intersect

crude: rough; not fully developed

culture: that which is excellent in the arts

current: the flow of a river

custom: a practice followed by certain people; the usual way of doing things

debate: a discussion where people with opposing points of view argue their points *debris:* scattered remains; garbage

delegate: someone who speaks and acts for a group of voters

destination: the place at the end of a journey

discourage: to persuade not to do something

discrimination: treating people unjustly because they are different

dismal: gloomy; sad

downstream: in the direction that a stream or river is flowing

draft: to select people for military service

economy: the production, use, value, and trade of materials within a state and country

ecosystem: a system formed by the interaction of organisms and their environment

efficient: effective and productive

elevated: raised up above the ground

Emancipation Proclamation: a document that freed the slaves, issued by Abraham Lincoln

empire: a group of countries under one ruler

employee: a person who works for wages

enchantment: delight

encourage: to give help to; to aid

enlist: to join the military

entrepreneur: a person who organizes, manages, and assumes the risk of a business

erosion: wearing away of the land by wind or water

ethnic: having to do with race or culture; having common traits and customs

expense: a cost; money spent

exposition: a public showing or exhibition

famine: a drastic food shortage

fertile: allowing lots of things to grow

fife: a small musical instrument like a flute

flint: a very hard stone that produces a spark

floodplain: the area along a river that is flooded

fluorite: a common mineral occurring in colored or clear crystals

forge: a furnace where metal is heated and worked

fossil: the print or remains of a plant or animal

free enterprise: a system where the people run businesses for profit, and where people buy and sell

frontier: a place at the edge of settled land

generator: a machine that produces electricity

gentry: upper-class people

geography: the study of the earth and the people, animals, and plants living on it

Gettysburg Address: a speech made by Abraham Lincoln to dedicate the national cemetery at Gettysburg, Pennsylvania

global: having to do with the whole world

goods: products that are made, bought, and sold

grain elevator: a building in which grain is stored

grid: a pattern where lines cross each other in even spaces

ground: to stop floating because the water is not deep enough

haunches: hips or hindquarters

heroic: brave and courageous

holocaust: destruction or devastation; the mass destruction of European Jews in Nazi concentration camps during World War II

idle: lazy; wasting time

immigrant: a person who moves into a new country

immoral: not moral; corrupt; unethical

independence: freedom from another's control or rule

Independent: a member of the Independent political party

Jesuit: a member of a Roman Catholic religious order for men

jury: citizens who decide a case in a courtroom

laureate: a person who receives an honor in his field

legend: a story passed down through the ages

legislator: a person elected to make laws

legislature: a body of people given the responsibility to make laws

local: near home

lock: an enclosure used in raising or lowering boats as they pass through different water levels

locomotive: an engine that hauls railroad cars

luxurious: elegant and extravagant

majority: a number greater than half

manufacture: to make something

massacre: the violent killing of a number of people

mica: a mineral that separates into layers

migration: movement from one country or place to another

military: the armed services (army, navy, air force, marines)

militia: people with military training who may serve in emergencies; a type of army

mission: a religious settlement

mortar: a mixture of cement that holds bricks together

negotiate: to discuss in order to come to an agreement

nominate: to choose someone to run as a candidate in an election

nutrient: something in the soil that makes it fertile

obstacle: something that blocks the way

official: authorized; approved

ordinance: a city rule or law

organism: a living person, animal, or plant

outhouse: an outdoor toilet

overseer: a person who watches over something

oversight: something that is left out; a mistake

pardon: to forgive a criminal

particle: a very small bit of something

pension: money paid by the government to a retired person

philanthropy: goodwill towards others, especially shown by giving to charities

plantation: a large farming estate

political: relating to government

politics: the activities of government or public affairs

population: the number of people living in an area

portage: to carry boats or goods overland from one body of water to another; a route for such carrying

precipitation: water that falls to earth as rain or snow

preserve: to save; to keep up and maintain

proclaim: to announce officially

product: something manufactured, thought, or grown

profit: the money made after expenses are paid

progress: advancement; forward movement

prohibit: to ban or forbid

prosperity: having success and economic good fortune

protective: guarding or caring for something

protest: a complaint or objection against an idea or action

radar: a system for sending out radio waves to track a ship or plane *ration:* to distribute food by government allowance

recite: to repeat from memory

recreation: activities done for fun

refine: to bring to a pure state

rendezvous: a big fair where trappers sold their furs

representative democracy: a form of government where a person is chosen to vote on behalf of other people

representative: a person elected to vote for other people

requirement: something that needs to be done or completed

reservation: an area of land where the U.S. government forced American Indians to live

reservoir: a place where water is stored for future use

resident: a person who lives in a place permanently

rival: competitor; a person who tries to equal or outdo another

rural: of the country; not in a city

salary: money paid to an employee

sap: sticky fluid inside trees

sapling: a young tree

savage: a person belonging to a primitive society

scour: to clean by rubbing or polishing

scouring: digging, scrubbing

seamstress: a woman who sews for a living

secede: to leave a country to form another country

segregate: to separate by race

service: something done for another person

shaman: a medicine man and religious leader

shell: a metal case holding the shot that is fired from a gun or cannon

slavery: the practice of owning another person like property

smallpox: a contagious disease that causes fever and scars the skin

sod: grass-covered ground

speculator: a person who determines the value of something

stock: money invested in a business

stockyard: a place where livestock are kept before they are slaughtered or shipped

strike: a protest where workers stop work until a change or agreement is made

surplus: an amount left over

surveyor: a person who measures and draws land for maps or other projects

synagogue: a Jewish house of worship

temperate: not excessive or extreme

tenement: a rundown, low-rental apartment building

thatch: straw and long grass woven together

tradition: a way of life handed down from parents to children

traditional: handed down from generation to generation

treaty: a formal agreement between two groups or countries

tributary: a stream flowing into a larger stream or a lake

union: an association of workers

urban: having to do with the city

valid: based on truth or fact

veto: to reject a bill; to say "no"

voyageur: a person who transported goods to and from trading posts

wage: money paid to employees

whitewash: to whiten a surface

wigwam: a hut made of poles overlaid with bark, rush mats, or hides

INDEX

A

A. Finkl & Sons Co., 193

Abbott Laboratories, 186, 196

Abbott, Robert, 142, 151

Abbott, Wallace D., 186, 196

Ackley, Mary E., 85

Addams, Jane, 127, 137

Africa, 77, 110

African Americans, 45, 56, 112, 120, 123, 140, 143, 147, 151, 152, 153, 154, 155, 159, 160, 164–165, 167, 169, 175, 180, 192

Allied Powers, 150

Alton, 112, 113, 118, 128, 150, 165

American Indians, 4, 12, 39–40, 46, 49, 50, 54, 55, 60, 61, 62–63, 65, 66, 67, 68, 69, 72, 73, 74, 80, 85, 88, 100, 128, 140, 191
villages, 47, 63
See also specific tribes

American War for Independence, 59, 64, 67, 73, 84

Amish, 95, 106

Ammon, Jakob, 106

animals, 4, 7, 10, 11, 12, 13, 17, 21, 23, 31, 32, 37, 39, 40, 41, 66, 67, 74, 75, 86, 87, 104, 111, 129, 150, 178, 181, 190, 196

beaver, 49, 51, 191
fur, 47, 48, 49, 51, 52, 54, 57, 73, 130
horses, 74, 84, 85, 98, 106, 133, 138, 141, 149
hunting, 29, 34, 35, 36, 49, 54
Ice Age, 22
livestock, 9, 18, 53
wild, 18, 28, 30
See also birds

Appalachian Mountains, 30, 31, 62, 65

archaeology, 29, 30, 32

Archaic people, 26, 29

Archer Daniels Midland, 196

architecture/architects, 135–136

Arcola, 106

Armstrong, Louis, 151, 153

army, 79, 100, 120, 122

Art Institute of Chicago, The, 136

Arthur, 106

Asia/Asians, 140, 144, 159, 166, 198

Atlantic Ocean, 63, 67, 84, 187, 195

Atwood, 106

Aurora, 144, 149

Austria-Hungary, 150

Autobiography of Black Hawk, The, 92

automobiles, 106, 130, 131, 142, 143, 149, 155, 163, 178, 188

B

Bell, Alexander Graham, 148

Belleville, 150

Bellow, Saul, 169

Bible, The, 91

Bickerdyke, Mary Ann, 121

Bill of Rights, The, 174

birds, 10, 12, 17, 31, 37

Bishop Hill, 95, 101

Black Hawk, 91–92

Black Hawk War, 83, 91–92, 100

blacks. See African Americans

Bloomington, 128

boats, 12, 65, 77, 78, 84, 86–87, 94, 96–98, 100, 104, 115, 123, 128, 138, 145, 153, 160, 166

Bond, Shadrach, 78, 79

Boone County, 76

Booth, John Wilkes, 123

Bourbonnais, 100

Bridgeport, 103

Brooks, Gwendolyn, 169

Brown County, 167

Burroughs, Edgar Rice, 169

business, 96, 99, 102, 106, 126, 128, 130–132, 135, 145, 146, 147, 148, 149, 155, 156, 162, 163, 174, 178, 181, 182, 188–194, 198

Byrne, Jane, 159, 167, 179

C

Cahokia, 27, 31, 32–33, 44, 49, 50, 197

Cahokia Indians, 34, 74

Cairo, 15, 96, 97, 121, 122, 123, 128

Camp Grant, 150, 160

Camp Robert Smalls, 160

Canada/Canadians, 4, 46, 47, 48, 51, 52, 60, 62, 72, 100, 111, 195

canals, 19, 78, 102–104, 114, 127, 128, 138, 145, 195

canoes, 46, 52, 57, 128

Capone, Al, 151

Carbondale, 165, 194

Carroll County, 76

cars. *See automobiles*

Carthage, 100

Cavelier, René-Robert. *See La Salle*

Cedarville, 137

Central Lowland, 14

Central Powers, 150

Centralia, 105, 128, 194

Champaign, 194

Chanute Training Field, 158

Charleston, 118, 178

Chester, 112

Chicago, 4, 7, 8, 24, 44, 49, 59, 67–68, 73, 74, 76, 98, 101, 103, 104, 112, 120, 126–141, 142, 143, 144, 148, 150, 152, 153, 156, 158, 159, 160, 165, 167, 168, 169, 179, 180, 181, 187, 192, 193, 194, 195, 196, 197

Chicago Bears, 140, 151

Chicago Blackhawks, 140

Chicago Board of Trade, 186, 197

Chicago Bulls, 140, 197

Chicago Cubs, 138, 140

Chicago Daily Defender, 151

Chicago Defender, 142, 151, 169

Chicago Heights, 150

Chicago Iron Company, 130

Chicago Opera Company, 136

Chicago Public Library, The, 136

Chicago River, 19, 67, 73, 126, 127, 128, 133, 138, 195

Chicago Symphony Orchestra, The, 136

Chicago Tribune, The, 134

Chicago White Sox, 140

China/Chinese, 144, 166

Chippewa Indians, 74

Cicero, 160

civil rights, 159, 164–165

Civil War, The, 109, 114, 116, 119–124

Civilian Conservation Corps (CCC), 156

Clark, George Rogers, 59, 65–66, 67, 84

Clark, William, 66

climate, 7, 9, 21, 22, 23, 32

clothing, 35, 39, 42, 49, 51, 54, 60, 63, 88, 120, 155, 163

coal, 14, 18, 20, 21, 23, 96, 97, 104, 105, 130–132, 154, 155, 176, 195

Collinsville, 32

Columbus, Christopher, 46, 136

Compton, Arthur, 162

computers, 18, 147, 159, 183, 198

Confederacy, The, 119–120, 122–124

Congress, 72, 76, 78, 79, 147

constitution, 76–78, 159, 174, 176–177, 182

Cook County, 76

Cook, Daniel Pope, 76

corn, 8, 9, 14, 18, 31, 35, 36, 37, 39, 42, 54, 104, 106, 128, 160, 179, 191, 193, 196, 197

cotton, 78, 111, 114, 124

Crenshaw, John Hart, 112

D

Daley, Richard M., 158, 181

Decatur, 115, 149, 160, 196

Declaration of Independence, The, 64, 164

Deere, John, 94, 98–99, 129, 192

DeKalb County, 76

Delaware Indians, 74

Democratic Party, 175

Des Plaines, 187, 193

Des Plaines River, 138, 195

Dickson Mounds, 31

disease, 100, 103, 193

Disney, Walt, 142, 148

Disneyland, 148

Dixon, 166

Dos Passos, John, 169

Douglas, Stephen A., 118, 119

Dreiser, Theodore, 169

DuPage County, 22, 76

Duryea, Charles, 142, 143

Du Sable, Jean Baptiste Point, 59, 67–68, 73, 126, 128

E

East St. Louis, 150, 154, 160

economy/economics, 114, 163, 166, 186–199

ecosystems, 10–11

Edgar, Jim, 178

education/schools, 69, 77, 90–91, 106, 111, 115, 132, 134, 137, 145, 156, 161, 162, 164, 168, 170, 174, 175, 176, 178, 180, 181, 182, 183, 184, 188, 192, 198

Edwards, Ninian, 72, 74

Eisenhower, Dwight, 163

Elgin, 144

Ellington, Duke, 151

Ellis Island, 145

Emancipation Proclamation, 109, 116, 123

energy, 8, 20

England/English, 37, 46, 47, 58, 59, 60–67, 69, 70, 74, 75, 92, 100, 137, 140, 144, 150, 162

entrepreneurs, 191–193

environment, 7, 10, 18, 19, 23, 170

Equal Rights Amendment (ERA), 165

Erie Canal, 102

Erie, Lake, 63

Europe/Europeans, 37, 46, 47, 49, 50, 51, 84, 96, 100, 105, 128, 135, 144, 146, 150, 151, 155, 160, 162

Evanston, 165

explorers, 12, 37, 46–49

F

Fales, Mary L., 133

farmers/farming, 9, 12, 14, 15, 16, 17, 18, 31, 34, 35, 39, 49, 54, 67, 79, 89, 94, 98–99, 100, 102, 106, 114, 116, 123, 128, 129, 140, 150, 155, 156, 170, 176, 178, 181, 183, 187, 191, 192, 193, 196, 197
  crops, 9, 18, 30, 36, 54, 74, 78, 84, 88, 99, 100, 104, 114, 123
  farms, 4, 32, 56, 78, 83, 90, 115, 118, 130, 131, 145, 146, 150, 160, 196

Ferris, George, 136

Ferris wheel, 136

Field, Marshall, 126, 130–131, 135, 192

Field Museum of Natural History, 130, 139

Finkl, Anton, 193

fire, Great Chicago, 126, 133–135, 193

fish, 10, 11, 12, 19, 29, 36, 39, 88, 169

fluorite, 21, 130

Ford, Henry, 143, 149

Ford's Theater, 116

forests, 7, 11, 21, 23, 115, 176

Fort Crevecoeur, 44, 48

Fort de Chartres, 44, 45, 49

Fort Dearborn, 70, 73, 74

Fort Dearborn Massacre, 70, 74, 82, 128

Fort Frontenac, 48

Fort Kaskaskia, 50

Fort Massac, 50, 64

Fort St. Louis, 44, 48, 49

Fort Sumter, 120, 124

Fort Wayne, 74

forts, 47, 48, 49, 50, 60, 63, 65, 120

Fox Indians, 27, 37, 74, 91–92, 181

Fox River, 37, 181

France/French, 37, 44, 45, 46, 47, 48, 49, 50, 51, 53, 54, 55, 56, 60–62, 63, 65, 66, 67, 69, 100, 150

Franklin County, 154

Freeman, Bud, 153

Freeport, 118, 128

French and Indian War, 58, 60–61

Fulton, Robert, 96

G

Galena, 21, 101, 104, 122, 128

Galena River, 56

Galesburg, 118, 121, 136, 168

General Assembly, 78, 131, 176–178

geography, 4–25

Germany/Germans, 140, 144, 150, 162, 191, 193

Gettysburg Address, 109, 116

glaciers, 14, 21–23, 28

Glenview, 196

Goodman, Benny, 151, 153

government, 4, 165
British, 62, 63
European, 46, 144
Illinois, 78, 102, 108, 118, 172–185, 198
territorial, 72
United States, 59, 66, 68, 73, 91, 92, 114, 122, 150, 156, 162, 172–185

Grand Detour, 99

Grange, Red, 151

Grant, Ulysses S., 122

Great Britain/British. *See England/English*

Great Depression, 143, 155–156, 160

Great Lakes, 8, 23, 47, 48, 63, 130, 187, 195

Great Lakes Naval Training Station, 150, 160

Great Migration, 143, 151

Greece/Greeks, 140, 144, 191

Gulf Coastal Plain, 15

Gulf of Mexico, 8, 30, 31, 44, 46, 48, 49, 102, 195

Gutierrez, Luis, 167

H

Haymarket Square Riot, 127, 132

Hemingway, Ernest, 169

Henry, Patrick, 65

Henson, Josiah, 110, 111

Hickory Hill, 112

highways/freeways, 21, 23, 156, 163, 176, 182, 183, 190, 194–195

Hispanics, 140, 159, 167

Hitler, Adolf, 162

Hodgers, Jennie, 120

holocaust, 162

Hopewell people, 31
Period, 27, 29, 30

Horseshoe Lake Fish and Wildlife Area, 15

House of Representatives, 108, 167, 174, 176–177

houses, 46, 49, 53, 54, 73, 88, 100, 101, 131, 133, 134, 137, 162, 163, 164, 170, 181, 182, 191, 194
Indian, 30, 33, 34, 35, 37, 48
slave, 111

sod, 16, 84

Hubbard, Gurdon, 129

Hull, Charles J., 137

Hull House, 127, 137

Hyde Park, 136

I

Ice Age, 21–22

Illini Indians, 27, 34–35, 37, 39, 48, 49, 55, 63

Illinois & Michigan Canal, 78, 95, 102–104, 186, 195

Illinois Central Railroad, 95, 104, 105

Illinois Herald, The, 70, 76, 78

Illinois River, 3, 12, 38, 78, 102, 103, 104, 160, 186, 195

Illinois Territory, 70, 72, 76

Illinois Waterway, 187, 195

Illinoisan Glacier, 22

immigrants, 100, 105, 128, 129, 137, 138, 140, 142, 144–146, 155, 166, 167, 191, 193

Independent Party, 175

Indiana, 65, 68, 74, 104, 108, 115

Indiana Territory, 70, 72

Indians. *See American Indians, specific tribes*

industry, 9, 21, 23, 78, 114, 128–132, 139, 146, 154, 176, 187, 192, 196, 197

insects, 86, 176

Interior Low Plateaus, 14

Iowa, 91, 92, 101
Ireland/Irish, 100, 103, 140, 144
iron, 15, 21, 130, 131, 195
Iroquois Indians, 37, 41
Italy/Italians, 140, 144, 145, 191

J

Jackson, Jesse, Jr., 174
Jackson Park, 136
Jansson, Eric, 101
Janssonists, 101
Japan/Japanese, 144, 158, 160, 166
Jazz Singer, The, 143
Jenney, William, 127, 135
Jo Daviess County, 76
Johnson County, 167
Johnson, George E., 192
Johnson Products, 187, 192
Joliet, 144, 150, 165
Joliet Iron and Steel Company, 130
Jolliet, Louis, 44, 46–47
Jonesboro, 118
Jungle, The (Sinclair), 129

K

Kane County, 76
Kankakee, 100,
Kaskaskia, 44, 47, 49, 50, 53, 55, 59, 65, 66, 67, 71, 72, 77, 78, 79, 83
Kaskaskia Indians, 34, 74

Kaskaskia River, 89
Kennedy, John F., 194
Kentucky, 65, 115
Kickapoo Indians, 27, 37, 74
King, B.B., 152
King, Martin Luther, Jr., 159, 164–165
Kinzie, John, 74
Korean War, 158, 166
Kroc, Ray, 193

L

La Salle, Sieur de, 44, 47–49
La Salle-Peru, 103
Lake County, 76
lakes, 4, 7, 10, 11, 18, 23, 34, 35, 39, 53, 63, 176
lead, 15, 21, 56, 101
Lee County, 76
Leiter, Joe, 154–155
Lewis, Meriwether, 66
limestone, 15, 21, 130
Lincoln, Abraham, 108–109, 115–120, 123, 124, 197
Lincoln-Douglas Debates, 109, 118
Lincoln, Mary Todd, 108, 116, 117, 119
Lincoln, Robert Todd, 116
Lincoln, Thomas, 115
Louisiana, 48, 176
Lovejoy, Elijah, 108, 113, 124
Lovejoy, Owen, 112, 113
Lowden, Esther, 42

M

manufacturing, 136, 150, 196
Marquette, Jacques, 44, 46–47
Marshall Field's, 130, 139
Massachusetts, 89, 130, 198
Masters, Edgar Lee, 169
Matoon, 194
Maywood, 165
McCormick, Cyrus, 94, 98, 99, 129, 132
McDonald's Corporation, 163, 187, 193
McHenry County, 76
Mennonite Church, 106
Meredosia, 104
Mexico/Mexicans, 144, 166, 167
Miami Indians, 37, 74
Michigamea Indians, 34, 74
Michigan, 65, 68
Michigan, Lake, 7, 8, 23, 37, 46, 67, 68, 73, 76, 78, 102, 103, 128, 130, 133, 136, 138, 154, 169, 181, 186, 194, 195
Milwaukee, 24, 195
minerals, 18, 21, 56, 75
mining, 14, 21, 56, 78, 101, 147, 154–155, 176, 191
miners, 20, 120, 131–132
Minnesota, 68, 130, 198
Mission of the Guardian Angel, 49
Mississippi Flyway, 10

Mississippi Palisades State Park, 13

Mississippi River, 12–13, 15, 23, 31, 37, 44, 46, 47, 48, 49, 50, 52, 54, 60, 66, 67, 76, 78, 91, 96–97, 100, 101, 115, 121, 123, 138, 153, 160, 168, 178, 187, 194, 195

Mississippian people, 31, 32 Period, 27, 29, 31

Missouri, 100, 113

Mitchell, Jeanette Pigsley, 84, 89

Moline, 99, 129, 150

Monks Mound, 32

Moody, Dwight L., 137

Mormons, 94, 100–101

Morris, Ernest, 151

Morton, Jelly Roll, 151

Moseley-Braun, Carol, 112, 175

Mound Builders, 31, 32, 34

mud slides, 23

Mueller, Hieronymus, 149

music/musicians, 97, 120, 143, 148, 151–153, 163, 168, 190

N

NAACP, 143, 147

Native Americans. *See American Indians, specific tribes*

natural resources, 21, 23, 60, 75, 192, 194

nature, 34, 39, 41, 169, 192

Nauvoo, 12, 94, 100–101

Navy Pier, 139

Nazis, 162

New Deal, 156, 160

New Orleans, 54, 60, 104, 115, 153

New Salem, 108, 115, 116–118

New World, 60

New York, 37, 100, 102, 114, 145, 147, 153

Northbrook, 196

Northern Cross Railroad, 104

Northwest Ordinance, 59, 69, 74

Northwest Territory, 59, 68–69, 72, 74, 84

Northwestern University, 180

O

Oak Brook, 163, 196

Oak Park, 169

Oak Street Beach, 4

Ogle County, 76

Ohio, 65, 68, 100, 106, 121, 122

Ohio River, 12, 15, 65, 76, 96, 121

oil, 18, 21, 23

Old Man and the Sea, The, 169

Old Slave House, 112

Oliver, Joe "King," 153

Orchard Place, 187, 194

Ottawa, 47, 118

Ottawa Indians, 63, 74

Ozark Mountains, 15

Ozark Plateau, 15

O'Hare, Edward, 194

O'Hare International Airport, 187, 194

O'Leary, Patrick, 133

P

Pacific Ocean, 66, 198

Paleo people, 26, 29

Palmer House, 135

Palmer, Potter, 135

Pearl Harbor, 158, 160

Pennsylvania, 93, 96, 104, 106

Peoria, 24, 44, 47, 48, 128, 150, 160, 166, 167, 196, 197

Peoria Indians, 34, 74

Peoria, Lake, 49

Persian Gulf War, 166

Piankesh Indians, 74

Pinet, Father Pierre François, 44, 49

pioneers, 12, 75, 80, 82–93, 181

plantations, 110, 111, 114

plants, 4, 7, 9, 10, 11, 17, 18, 20, 21, 22, 28, 29, 30, 34, 39, 66, 106

Poland/Polish, 144

political parties, 174, 175

Pontiac, 63

Pontiac's War, 58, 63

Pope County, 22

Pope, Nathaniel, 76

population, 71, 80, 179

Potawatomi Indians, 27, 37, 42, 67, 74, 181

prairie, 4, 7, 10, 11, 14, 16–17, 22, 28, 33, 34, 42, 84, 85, 89, 98, 101, 160

Prairie du Rocher, 45, 49

Princeton, 112

Proclamation Line of 1763, 58, 62 , 64

prohibition, 151

Prudential Building, 139

Pullman Company, 160

Pullman, George, 132

Pullman Strike, 127, 132

Q

Quincy, 112, 118, 128

R

railroads, 4, 21, 94, 100, 102, 104–105, 107, 114, 121, 123, 128, 129, 130, 131, 132, 134, 139, 145, 146, 162, 191, 194–195

Rantoul, 150

Reagan, Ronald, 166, 167

Red Cross, 150

Reed, Shirley, 40

religion, 31, 32, 39, 46, 47, 49, 53, 69, 100–101, 106, 144, 174

Renault, Philippe, 56

rendezvous, 51

Republican Party, 175

Revolutionary War. *See American War for Independence*

Ridgely, Nicholas, 104

rivers, 4, 6, 7, 9, 10, 11, 12, 18, 19, 21, 23, 24, 29, 30, 31, 34, 35, 39, 46, 47, 49, 50, 51, 52, 53, 63, 84, 85, 86, 87, 88, 96, 102, 113, 128, 176, 195

roads, 82, 85, 102, 104, 106, 149, 163, 178, 194

Rock Island, 128, 150, 160

Rock River, 92

Rockford, 24, 112, 144, 150, 160, 167, 196

Roosevelt, Franklin, 156, 160

Root, George F., 120

Russia/Russians, 144, 146, 150

S

Sacajawea, 66

Sandburg, Carl, 168

Sandrovitch, Alvin, 146

Sanitary and Ship Canal, 138, 186, 195

Sauk Indians, 27, 37, 74, 91–92, 181

schools. *See education*

Sears and Roebuck, 131

Sears, Richard, 131

Sears Tower, 127, 139, 197

Selkirk, James, 149

Senate, 175, 176–177, 181

Seneca, 160

Sengstacke, John H., 151

settlers, 16, 37, 54, 69, 73, 74, 76, 80, 84, 88, 91, 94–107, 191, 194 *See also immigrants*

Shawnee National Forest, 14

ships, 52, 110, 128, 144, 145, 146, 150, 160, 161, 195, 198

Silurian Sea, 21

Sinclair, Upton, 129

slavery, 45, 56, 67, 69, 76, 77–78, 108–120, 123–124, 152, 153

smallpox, 63

Smith, Bessie, 152

Smith, Hyrum, 100

Smith, Joseph, 100

soldiers, 37, 60, 66, 73, 74, 92, 120–123, 150, 154, 160–162

soybeans, 8, 9, 18, 197

Spain/Spanish, 46, 47, 49, 140, 167

Springfield, 24, 71, 79, 83, 93, 104, 108, 109, 117, 128, 143, 147, 160, 165, 176, 179, 197

St. Charles, 181

St. Lawrence River, 47, 52

St. Lawrence Seaway, 52, 187, 195

St. Louis, 24, 66, 104, 113

stagecoaches, 103

Stagg Field, 162

Starr, Ellen, 137

Starved Rock, 38, 44, 48

Starved Rock State Park, 3, 38, 156

statehood, 70–71, 76–80, 83, 84, 176, 196

steel, 130, 135, 150, 193

Stephanson County, 76

stock market, 143, 155

Stockwell, Elisha, 122

sugar, 78, 111, 114, 115

Sullivan, 106

Sullivan, Louis, 135

Sultana, The, 123

Superior, Lake, 30, 31

Sweden/Swedish, 100, 101, 140, 144, 168

T

Tall Grass Prairie Region, 16

Tamaroa Indians, 34, 74

Tampico, 166

taxes, 178, 181, 182–183, 198

Taylor, Koko, 152

Tillson, Christiana Holmes, 89

Tonti, Henri de, 47–49

tools, 29, 30, 54, 55, 56, 98, 111, 129

tornadoes, 8–9, 23

transportation, 4, 19, 21, 31, 53, 102–105, 106, 136, 138, 149, 181, 194–195, 197

trappers/traders, 47, 49, 51, 52, 54, 62, 63, 67, 191

Treaty of Paris, 58

Tribune Building, 133

Twain, Mark, 12, 97

U

Underground Railroad, 109, 111–112

Union Stock Yard, 126, 129

unions, 119–124, 131–132, 147, 154–155

University of Chicago, 162

Utah, 101, 176

Utica, 44, 49

V

Vandalia, 71, 78, 79, 83, 88, 118

Vietnam/Vietnamese, 166

Vietnam War, 159, 166

Vincennes, 59, 65, 66, 72

Virden, 132

Virginia, 59, 65, 67, 68, 98, 114

voting, 76, 78, 137, 143, 174, 177, 184

voyageurs, 51, 52–53, 57

W

Wabash River, 37, 59, 66

wagons, 16, 84–86, 97, 101, 112, 114, 141, 149, 191

War of 1812, 70, 74, 79, 92

Ward, Montgomery, 126, 131

Washington, D.C., 116, 119, 123, 174, 175, 176, 179

Washington, Harold, 159, 167, 180

water, 4, 11, 12, 23, 24, 38, 39, 42, 53, 56, 73, 75, 76, 88, 96, 103, 110, 121, 128, 138, 146, 166, 170, 176, 178, 195

Wea Indians, 74

wheat, 8, 9, 54, 99, 104, 106, 128, 150, 168, 179, 191, 196, 197

White House, The, 119

White Pine Forest State Park, 10

Whiteside County, 76

Williams, Eugene, 154

Williamson County, 167

Winfrey, Oprah, 187, 192

Winnebago County, 76

Wisconsin, 46, 65, 68, 76, 104, 130, 176, 193

World War I, 143, 144, 150–151, 154, 155

World War II, 158–163, 166, 170, 194

World's Columbian Exposition, 127, 136

Wright, Frank Lloyd, 135

Wright, Richard, 169

Wrigley Building, 139

Wrigley Field, 138, 140

Y

Yates, Richard, 123

YMCA, 137

Young, Brigham, 101

Z

Zeigler, 154

CREDITS

ART

Burton, Jon 20

Maxwell, Matthew 8

Rasmussen, Gary viii, 1, 10, 11, 15, 28, 29, 30, 31, 34, 35 (upper), 36 (right), 39, 40, 41, 48 (left), 51, 52, 54, 57, 81, 86, 89, 147, 175, 190

PHOTOGRAPHS

A. Finkl & Sons Company 193 (right)

Academy of Motion Picture Arts and Sciences 166 (left)

Blanchette, David 7 (lower left), 10 (middle), 70, 79 (upper left), 172

Byrne, Jane, Office of 179

California Historical Society Library 148 (left)

Chicago Daily Defender 151, 153, 169 (lower), 192 (left)

Chicago Historical Society 67 (lower), 126, 128 (upper), 133, 134 (right), 136 (lower left, lower right)

Daley, Richard M., Office of 181 (right)

Deseret News 165, 166 (right)

Ernest Hemingway Foundation of Oak Park 169 (upper)

Field Museum, The 139 (lower right)

Frank Lloyd Wright Home and Studio Foundation, The 135 (upper right)

Harold Washington Library Center, Chicago Public Library 180

Hirsch, Karen I. 7 (lower right), 9 (all), 10 (lower), 14 (lower), 16 (right), 19, 50 (lower), 52, 60 (all), 64, 79 (upper right), 101 (right), 106 (all), 116, 117 (middle), 136 (upper left), 139 (left inset), 140 (lower left)

Illinois Historic Preservation Agency 16 (left inset), 20, 29, 31, 33 (all), 38 (all), 44, 50 (upper), 58, 66, 67 (upper middle), 79 (middle left), 82, 85 (upper), 92 (left), 117 (insets), 118 (upper left, right, inset), 163 (lower)

Illinois Historical Society Library 53

Illinois State Historical Library 37 (upper), 46, 48 (right), 49, 55, 56 (upper), 67 (right), 73, 76, 77, 79 (upper right), 79 (lower right), 86 (all), 94, 96, 97 (left), 98 (all), 99 (all), 100, 103, 109 (inset), 113, 115 (lower), 120 (all), 121, 122 (lower left), 129, 132, 134 (left), 142, 150, 156 (upper), 158, 160, 168

Illinois State Museum 37 (lower)

Ivanko, John D. 4, 7 (upper right), 8, 12 (all), 14 (upper), 23, 75 (left), 97 (right), 101 (left), 127 (inset), 130 (right), 135 (lower left, lower right), 139 (middle, right inset, upper right), 140 (left, middle right, upper right), 152, 167, 193 (lower right), 197 (lower)

Jackson, Jesse Jr., Office of 174

Kansas State Historical Society, Topeka 90 (upper)

LDS Archives 144

Lynn, John 13 (all), 16 (background), 17 (all), 75 (right), 85 (lower), 88, 92 (right), 118 (lower left), 125, 128 (lower), 186, 195, 197 (upper)

Marshall Field's 130 (left)

McDonald's Corporation 193 (left)

Michigan Department of State Archives 35 (lower), 145 (left), 164

Minnesota Historical Society 39

Ohio Historical Society 63, 65, 90 (lower)

Peale Museum, Baltimore 146

Pohn, Alison 138 (left)

Skrebneski, Harpo Productions, Inc. 192 (right)

St. Charles CVB 181 (left)

Till, Tom 2, 15 (all), 32

United States Senate 175

University of Illinois at Chicago, The University Library, Jane Addams Historical Collection 137

Utah State Historical Society 161

Wyoming State Archives 147, 155

MAPS by Alaine Sweet

All photographs not listed are from the collection of Gibbs Smith, Publisher.